MASTER YOUR CAREER PLAYBOOK:

RESUMES

Your Cheat Sheet to Writing Resumes

Sarahi,
I pray that you will succeed beyond measure in all that you set out to accomplish!!! Allow your natural curiosity to guide you and may it lead you to fulfill the purpose that you were created to achieve!!! Never allow anyone to tell you that something is impossible because the word alone tells you that IMPOSSIBLE!! May you become all that you desire to be and more!!

Juanita Hines

Juanita
JH
Jer 29:11-13
7/13/16

Master Your Career Playbook: Resumes
© November 2015
By Juanita L. Hines, Regional Consulting

Disclaimer

All the material contained in this book is provided for educational and informational purposes only. No responsibility can be taken for any results or outcomes resulting from the use of this material.
While every attempt has been made to provide information that is both accurate and effective, the author does not assume any responsibility for the accuracy or use/misuse of this information.

Cover art courtesy of: Will Norwood
Interior layout by: Melissa@TheWriterLab.com

Printed in the United States of America
First Printing, 2015

ISBN 978-0-9968090-0-9

Regional Consulting
PO Box 54
Fresno, TX 77545

www.regionalconsult.com

ACKNOWLEDGEMENTS

I would like to thank all the people who helped me throughout the birthing process of this book and those who stuck in there with me and provided encouragement when I needed it most!! Your encouragement did not fall on deaf ears and I am truly grateful for each and every one of you!!

Sending special thanks to Lisa Jammer, LaMetrice Dopson, Donald Hatter, Antoine Bryant, Zawadi Bryant, Jennise Beverly Chaffold, Dylan Raymond, Jonathan Sprinkles, Delina Pryce McPhaull, Marcie Brooks, Michelle Ngome, Michael G. Davis, LaShanda Litaker, Nickea Bradley, Alisha Schoennagel, LaToshia Norwood, Will Norwood, Dr. Yul Everline, Mrs. T. Perry, Connie Berger, Velvet Jones, Kim Mason, Sherica Matthews and Melissa Scott for your hands-on assistance, advice, encouragement and feedback throughout this entire writing process.

Each of you were extremely instrumental in helping me to complete this book with your own individual input and I would not have completed this book without each one of you. In the event that I missed anyone, please charge it to my head and not my heart because I am grateful for every contribution that has been made- whether great or small!!

To the job seekers and professionals who will read this book, there are many books on writing resumes and I thank you for choosing this one! I hope that you will follow the advice provided and that you may obtain the career of your dreams.

Last but not least, thanks to my daddy, Alphonso Hines, for always encouraging me to pursue my goals, dreams and telling me that anything is possible if you put your mind to it! I love you now more than ever, but not as much as tomorrow.

CONTENTS

PRE-GAME ANALYSIS

As a former athlete and someone who has always been impassioned with competitive sports, I understand the importance of making sure you are equipped with all the tools you need in order to succeed.

One commonality between almost every competitive team sport is that coaches utilize playbooks to maintain their arsenal of plays. The playbooks contain different strategies and unique plays that are customized in hopes of favorably positioning their team over the competition.

Playbooks are essential to the success of a team and having access to another team's plays in advance can give a strong advantage over the competition.

"Master Your Career Playbook: Resumes" is your cheat sheet or 1-on-1 guide to writing resumes that will help you position yourself for professional success. My goal is to help YOU gain a competitive advantage over other job seekers and attract the attention of recruiters and hiring managers.

Your resume is one of the most important documents that will help determine your career path, help you paint your story and define your destiny! That's a strong statement, I know... Allow me to explain.

You've probably heard that a person has less than 20 seconds to capture the attention of a hiring manager or recruiter. That statement, in most cases, is true. Nowadays, however, there are Applicant Tracking Systems (ATS) — software systems that scan resumes to identify candidates who best align with job qualifications based on hiring metrics—they can eliminate your resume before an actual recruiter even has an opportunity to review it.

With more than 10 years' experience working within the area of Human Resources with a specialization in recruiting and consulting, I have been responsible for sourcing and hiring individuals on all levels of the employment spectrum, both domestically and globally. I've had the opportunity to place individuals in positions ranging from entry-level office support, clerical and administrative positions to engineers, management and senior-level executive/ C-Suite positions.

Throughout my recruiting tenure, I have reviewed resumes, interviewed and hired candidates within various industries and have also placed candidates within Fortune 500 and non-profit, government contracting and Oil & Gas companies.

Because of this vast experience, I am confident that the information in this book will help you transform your resume and get you moving in the right direction. In this book, I will share the biggest mistakes people make, as well as highlight best practices. More importantly, I will coach you through the process of developing your resume while also providing you with insight into the recruiting process.

While there are countless opinions from recruiters on what should and should not go on a resume and how it should look (layout, design, etc.), there is one thing on which majority of recruiters and hiring managers can agree... content! The discussion of content will be the focal point of this book.

When most people write resumes, what they typically give you is a complete regurgitation of their experience, meaning that they list every single thing they've done. Then they leave it up to the recruiter or resume reviewer to determine what skills and experience is most relevant to the position which they have applied.

WRONG!

I want to help you get it right!

This book is a powerful guide, packed with information that will provide insight on how to more effectively articulate your experience. It will guide you through the process and help you land interviews that will lead to your desired position.

This is not a sit-down-by-the-pool-to-read type of book. This book will require your full, pen-in-hand participation. I purposely designed this book to be task-oriented so you will have an opportunity to apply the concepts immediately.

Oftentimes, people begin projects with a great amount of momentum and motivation, however, by the time they finish reading the "how-to guide", the energy they began tackling the task with has dissipated and the task remains undone.

I want to empower you with knowledge, but also the opportunity to implement the new strategies in a timely manner.

My goal is that you will actively participate and engage while reading this book by answering the questions and following prompts. If you follow the instructions I lay out, by the time you finish reading this book, your resume will be complete—ready to submit to your dream job.

Please do not skip chapters, exercises or half-do steps and make sure that you are as thorough as possible.

By the time you finish reading this book, your resume will not only be updated, but it will sell your skills and experience better than any prior resume that you have constructed.

More often than not, by the time people consult with me about their job search, they are extremely frustrated and fatigued because they feel as if they have tried everything to find a job and improve their marketability.

What they're doing is not working. They sometimes feel as if they have done all of the leg work possible to make their resume appealing, but their job search has stalled.

In my consulting, I have helped clients break through the roadblocks and I will do the same for you!

Just follow the process. Should you get stuck, I will gladly serve as a resource. In the event that you get tripped up or have additional questions that are not already covered in the book, feel free to send me your questions on TWITTER and tag me using @RegionalConsult or on Facebook at Regional.Consulting!

When I founded Regional Consulting in 2006, I wanted to empower individuals with tools, knowledge and insight that would help them succeed in their professional endeavors by providing open and honest professional development training. One of the most essential elements that I committed to when I started this company was the obligation to always be honest with my clients; which is where the tagline "Realism–When You Need to Know" was derived.

You can expect this book to be straight-forward. I will tell you what you need to know in order to succeed, even at the risk of you putting the book down and walking away.

I urge you to stick with me until the end, even through the times that do not necessarily make sense. I might ask you to do things that seem tedious or time consuming and there may be times when you may not like me very much. But stick with me. In the end, when those recruiting calls start coming in, you'll love me again.

Anthony Robbins said, "If you do what you've always done, you will get what you've always gotten." Isn't it time to try something new?

If written properly, your resume can open doors to jobs that align with your career goals, objectives, interests and/or passions and I look forward to coaching you through the process.

So find a spot where you can read and let's start working on creating your resume that will lead to the career of your dreams.

It's time to begin creating your Career Playbook starting with your resume!! It's GAME TIME!!!

Juanita Hines

July 2015

1ˢᵗ QUARTER STRATEGY: ESTABLISHING THE GAME PLAN

One of the things I find most amazing about sports is that on any given day, the "Goliath" can be beaten.

As was the case when my college football team, Appalachian State, unexpectedly stunned the University of Michigan at their stadium in 2007, which has since been hailed as one of the greatest upsets in college football history.

The defeat was a devastating blow not only to the psyche of their students, but it also forced the Wolverines from their 5ᵗʰ place national ranking to being pushed out entirely of the AP Poll.

Despite the fact that the game occurred more than eight years ago and Michigan has since taken their revenge on our school, the damage was already done.

I was present last weekend when a Texas A&M graduate referenced the game to another A&M alumni while watching college football at a local pub in Houston, TX. Unbeknownst to either of them, an Appstate Mountaineer was in their presence.

As I think back on how our team was able to achieve victory in that game, I realize that a large part of our success was due to the game plan Coach Moore had in place. The game plan is your blueprint to success and will be the thing you consult when unexpected things occur.

Such is the case in your professional life as well; you should have a game plan that will help you achieve success and your resume is one of those components.

Before we can begin trying to customize your resume as a part of your playbook; we must first come to a mutual understanding and agreement on a few major concepts that will hopefully change how you view your resume.

Let's start by first establishing a mutual agreement on the purpose of a resume. What do you think is the purpose of a resume?

Most people think the purpose of a resume is to get you the job....

WRONG!

Simplifying the Purpose

Regardless of the level of your career, the purpose of your resume is not to *get* you the job, but to get you the *interview* so that you can get the job!

The importance of understanding this distinction can make the difference between getting a phone interview and an in-person interview vs. getting your resume "placed on file" or receiving an automatic response stating that you are "unqualified for the position."

Your resume is your marketing tool that serves to sell and promote your relevant experience and it entices the recruiter or hiring manager to ask you in for an interview. Your resume will often precede you for majority of the positions which you will apply.

The interview is where you will have the opportunity to speak more in-depth regarding your background and experience as well as why you're potentially the best candidate for the position.

Dispelling Resume Myths

Myth #1 - List everything

Many job seekers feel their resume should be comprised of ALL of their professional experience. This is a myth.

When people write their resumes, they oftentimes try to force every single thing that they have done within all of their professional jobs on the resume—without regard to relevance. By doing so, they are doing themselves a disservice because they may have phenomenal experience that is very closely aligned with what the employer is seeking, but employers may not take enough time to identify why they're the best fit.

Let me explain it another way.

I oftentimes feel as if I am an anomaly, because, as a woman, I am not a fan of shopping! I get frustrated when I have to shop for clothes, furniture or pretty much anything other than food. On the other hand, I have friends who can shop for hours; carelessly trying on clothes to find the perfect dress or shoes while going from store to store for hours upon hours.

When I have to shop, I like to go to stores that place the clothes that I can potentially see myself in, on mannequins directly in front of the corresponding outfits. Why? Because when I find what I like, I want to go straight to it. I sometimes get frustrated and quickly lose heart when I have to go through clutter and congested racks to find clothes or even worse, take the time to actually go through the racks and find the perfect dress, only to discover that it's not available in my size.

Recruiters are the same way. They don't want to take the time to sift through all of the clutter in your resume to find out if you're a valuable fit. It's up to you to market yourself the right way and make yourself stand out. Be the well-dressed mannequin. Don't make them work too hard to figure out that they want to invite you to an interview.

Myth #2 – The Longer the Better

Some people think that longer resumes sell you better and make you stand out more because pages and pages demonstrates vast experience and are an indication of tremendous experience.

As a former recruiter, I have had countless occasions where candidates presented resumes that listed every single thing they had done (Myth #1) resulting in three–and four-page resumes for someone with less than three years professional experience.

I've heard individuals confess that they think a longer resume means you're better qualified. That's simply not true.

When I assisted my clients with resume writing, one of the first questions I asked them was: *would you read this three or four-page resume?* Usually, they would respond with a resounding, "Yes!" I realized that they were still emotionally attached to their resume and no one, at first, wants to admit that theirs is wrong.

Next, I would take a piece of paper and either cover their name or write a generic name atop of the resume and I would ask the question again, "NOW, would you read it?" More often than not, they gave a more honest and humble "No" response.

"Why not?" I would ask. After being able to pull themselves away from the "work of their own hands," they would provide me with honest answers:

It's WAY too long!
It's boring.
It's generic.
It's bland.

Longer does not mean better—it just means there is more to read.

While there may be value for some in having a one-page resume, a two-page resume can be most beneficial for others; however, you must find the balance because you do not want your resume to be too long nor do you want it to be too short and not contain sufficient information.

Myth #3 – Go Keyword Crazy

I've witnessed job seekers randomly inputting keywords into their resumes so that their resumes will successfully make it through the Applicant Tracking System (ATS). But throwing in random keywords without any supporting detail is not going to make your resume any more attractive to a recruiter, hiring manager or even an ATS. Operating by that theory is like expecting that a trip to the grocery store will satisfy your appetite even if you don't buy or eat any food there.

ATS systems not only look for keywords, but they also observe the contextual utilization of the specific keywords. The quality of the content should make your resume stand out and your usage of keywords should be relative to your experience.

When you input keywords, you should effectively match what the employer is seeking with your experience (we will cover keywords more extensively in chapter 5).

There are countless other resume blunders, but I wanted to focus on these three because they are some of the most common mistakes I've witnessed. I want you to be aware of them from the start so that you will avoid these as we work to build your resume.

Trying on New Shoes

So far we've learned that a resume is your tool for landing an interview, and we've dispelled the myths that loaded, long and keyword-stuffed resumes are effective. Now let's get into the thick of creating your marketing tool.

Before starting your resume process, I would like for you to indulge in an exercise for a moment.

Imagine you are a recruiter for a growing company and you're in the market to hire a salesperson, which candidate would you prefer to interview and possibly hire?

Candidate A states on his resume that he has 15 years of direct industry sales experience

Candidate B states on his resume that he has four years of business-to-business corporate sales experience in which he has more than tripled sales within the past two years, incrementally increasing customer sales from $300,000 to more than $1.2 million dollars annually

Based only on the information that has been provided above, which candidate would you prefer to bring in for an interview?

It may not seem fair to judge or base interview invitations without any additional insight into the candidate's personality or overall fit for the position. But without having any additional information that differentiates candidates or supporting details, outside of the content within the resume, recruiters are tasked with making these difficult choices every day.

As you write your resume, remember to put yourself in the shoes of the recruiter or hiring manager.

Next, imagine you are the same recruiter and you receive hundreds of resumes for one sales job; how will you differentiate between the candidates?

Your client wants the salesperson to start ASAP. This is only one of several clients that you support and you have a number of other positions that you urgently need to fill as well. You have some very difficult choices in front of you.

How much time do you think you can dedicate to this one particular search? How many resumes will you read through? How many candidates will you call and follow-up with? How many are you going to bring in for interviews? How will you decide which candidates to interview?

Let me help you answer those questions. While the choices would be difficult to make, you would review the resumes you received and find the candidates who were able to best articulate their experience on paper and those who took the time to make it most relatable to you and the position which you are currently hiring. There is a chance that you could have phone screens with 20 individuals, but varying by your team and resources, you would narrow down the candidates based on best overall company fit. You would also work with your client to decide which candidate to hire.

You must try to understand life from a recruiter's perspective and tailor your resume accordingly.

To those who may have had negative experiences in the past with recruiters, do not allow that to hold you back from your future or dissuade you from applying for other opportunities. Recruiters aren't lazy; they just have many competing pressures and demands they face daily. While you may feel it is easy to call one candidate back, imagine having eight hours in the day to respond to more than 300 candidates while interviewing, following-up with clients, building new client relationships and more responsibilities.

I'm sharing this insight with you because the easier you make it for the recruiter to say "Yes" to your resume, the better off you will both be.

When a departmental or organizational need arises, more often than not, the position has usually been vacant for quite some time. Filling the position might have gotten placed on the backburner. So, more often than not, by the time they contact a recruiter, employers are in desperate need for the position to be filled. These circumstances create pressure and a sense of urgency to find and identify great potential candidates expeditiously.

The value of the ATS

How much time can a recruiter devote to one search? That depends on the workload they currently have as well as their availability of resources, such as a database of readily available candidates that may have been previously screened, number of staff, referrals, recruiting budget and additional available resources that may be at their disposal.

From posting the position to screening candidates through phone and in-person interviews, all of these steps require time. This is when the ATS truly comes in handy because after posting a position, recruiters are oftentimes bombarded with candidates who will range from very highly qualified to drastically underqualified.

There have been numerous times when I placed ads for one available position online and in less than a 2 hour period, I received more than 200 resumes! This is one of the benefits of the ATS and one of the reasons why they are so valuable. Applicant Tracking systems help recruiters reduce the clutter and congestion of resumes that do not appear to be qualified—which directly relates to the earlier point of strategically utilizing keywords and relating your skills to the position to garner appropriate attention.

By building your resume with this book, you will learn how to make it past the ATS, and also learn how to best customize your resume so that you can garner the attention of the person with the power to grant you an interview.

Human resources professionals want to find the best candidates who most closely align with client or organizational desires while using the least amount of time necessary. The job search process can be much easier for you when you step into the recruiter's shoes. Make it easy for recruiters to see your value so that you can get hired.

Chapter Recap

In this chapter, we explained the importance of a resume, challenges that recruiters and hiring managers face as well as why it is important to make your experience relevant to the employer.

Now that you have completed this chapter you should have:

✓ A good grasp on the TRUE purpose of a resume
✓ More complete understanding of the difficult choices and decisions recruiters are faced with daily and why it's important for you to put in a little extra effort
✓ A better understanding of the value and purpose of the Applicant Tracking System (ATS) as well as what it is seeking

2ND QUARTER STRATEGY: REVIEWING PAST PERFORMANCE

Know Where You Stand

If you were to ask me, I think one of the main keys to success for any team is having a full understanding of your strengths and weaknesses, as well as those of your opponent. The best and most successful coaches learn how to play to their team's strengths while exposing their opponent's weaknesses.

One of the first things coaches do to prepare for their upcoming opponent is review tape of their team's prior games as well as tape of their opponent. They may also watch tape of the last time the teams competed against each other to see where majority of the errors occurred, evaluate the effectiveness of plays, identify where weaknesses existed and what could have been done to improve the team's performance, without regard to the outcome (whether they won or lost).

Just as any coach in competitive sports needs to know where their team stands to position themselves over the competition; you should also know where you stand as a professional in your own career.

So, grab a notebook and get cozy because, depending on just how much experience you possess, we may be here for a while.

I traditionally recommend that people use old-fashioned pen and paper because it may help when you recall information quickly and information begins to flood your memory. Most people write faster than they type; however if the opposite is true for you, do what suits you best. You are welcomed to make notes on your laptop, tablet or phone.

Additionally, I would recommend throughout the remainder of this process that you try to limit your time in these tasks to no more than four hours within one sitting, as I want to ensure that you do not get burned out or frustrated with the process and quit prematurely.

Assessing your experience

Now, for each of the positions that you've held over the past 10-15 years (or whatever time period specified for your particular industry), answer these questions:

o   What was my job? What did I do?
o   What did I achieve?
o   What did I enjoy doing?
o   What were some things I did not enjoy doing?
o   Based on that job, is there anything I know I don't want to do—whether now or in the future?

Let's tackle each of those questions one-by-one.

What was my job/ What did I do?

This section is not simply limited to your job title. Include all of your responsibilities and things you did that may not necessarily have been listed in your official job description. For example, when working with clients that may have worked in sales, they often fail to mention the relationship cultivation and retention duties they performed, because it was almost second-nature to them.

Remember that this will not be a quick process. This is not a section that you can complete in 10 minutes. Make sure you provide as much detail as possible.

I've found that, with my clients, this was the most time consuming and grueling part of the process. Many found it challenging to remember exactly what they had done within specific roles, especially when significant time had elapsed.

After you begin to identify the larger roles you had, start breaking down the details of the tasks. To help you get started on this portion of the process, here are some additional questions that you can ask yourself:

- o How did I do this task?
- o What resources was I given? How did I acquire them?
- o What tasks were required of me on a regular basis?
- o Whom did I support in performing this task?
- o How many people did I support in this role?
- o What were the unwritten responsibilities and expectations?
- o What was I held accountable for within my role?

o   What were some of the duties I did without recognition or being asked?

o   Did I manage or supervise anyone? If so, how many people? In what tasks did I oversee them? How did I evaluate them?

o   Was I responsible for performance reviews? Counseling? Hiring? Terminating?

o   How did we come up with ideas within the department?

o   Who managed my calendar? Or did I manage someone else's calendar?

o   Did I have any fiduciary responsibilities?

This is a small list of questions and is not intended to be comprehensive; however, feel free to utilize this starter list as your springboard to trigger your memory.

In the event that you have old performance reviews, this would be a great time to pull them out to see the areas in which you were (or are) being evaluated.

You should write as much detail as you can remember. Keep in mind that there is no task too great or too small and should include even the most mundane tasks, which could be anything— from taking out the trash, escorting people to their tables at a restaurant, clearing paper jams, managing a team of employees on unrelated tasks or planning your company gatherings.

What did I Achieve?

Let's go back to the earlier example of the recruiter reviewing the two candidates in the previous chapter. You may have noticed that the second person was much more effective in gaining your interest because he was able to demonstrate results he achieved.

The key to having an effective resume and getting interviews is demonstrating how what you have done can potentially be replicated. It's up to you to communicate how you can potentially achieve those results or better within their company or organization. That's what recruiters and hiring managers really want to know.

When you think back on the things you were able to achieve within your past experience, what are the things that stand out? Here are a few questions to begin the process of jogging your memory:

- How many accounts did you manage? Did you do so simultaneously?
- What were the prior sales before you took over the account?
- Did your organization have an influx of customers due to actions on your part?
- How many people did you successfully hire or manage?
- How many people were you able to positively impact?
- Did you help construct a plan or program that is now being utilized throughout the organization?
- What information can you potentially quantify within your role? Sales? People? Budgetary management? Savings? Returns on investments?
- Did you implement any processes that improved employee morale or reduced turnover in your department?
- Have you done anything that exceeded standards and expectations?
- Were you able to help optimize production? If so, how?
- How were you able to save the company money or reduce overhead costs?

o How many people did you train who went on to become successful?

o Did you serve as a mentor to other individuals that garnered positive results?

o Were any of your efforts, projects or ideas recognized or awarded, whether through your organization, media, clients or other parties?

One of the most important tasks you must do is identify how the tasks you have completed have impacted the lives of others within the organization, your internal and external constituents, customers, etc.

Even small numbers add up. It may not seem like very much to you, but when you add the numbers up, they can sometimes produce large contributions you've overlooked or simply taken for granted.

For example, imagine that you came up with a process that helped alleviate bottlenecks in the production line, which resulted in the production of 30 additional units per hour. Over the course of an eight-hour work day, that could mean producing an extra 240 units a day; which adds up to an additional 1200 units per week and more than 62,400 units per year! If your company sold the units for even $2 (which is a bare-bones figure), that adds up to more than $124,800! Imagine if the company sold the units for $20. That adds up to almost $1.2 million in additional revenue and that's just the amount of the surplus which resulted from a simple solution you created!

Do you see how small individual contributions can add up to larger sums?

You may find that this is the most difficult thing for you to recall. People often minimize their accomplishments and find it easier to remember things for which they may have been reprimanded or did not perform well. My goal though this book is to help change your mentality and thought process when it comes to your contributions.

Let's say you're an accountant or an accounting manager and you've identified and implemented software that not only helped perform tasks faster and reduced errors, but also saved time and cost less in administrative fees. Without the software, how much time and man-hours would you have used trying to identify and correct the errors that had been made? Is the process more simplified and less time consuming to check?

As I mentioned in the earlier point, you should make sure to check out your performance reviews because they will typically contain information on your accomplishments that you may have forgotten about or glossed over.

Don't worry... this problem happens to the best of us!

When looking at my own experience, within several of my client sites, I was able to successfully renegotiate vendor fees and partnership agreements that several of the organizations had with staffing agencies. I also alleviated redundancies in software and recruiting sites; which drastically reduced unnecessary expenditures and resulted in cost savings of tens of thousands of dollars for my clients.

It was not until after I reviewed my own performance evaluations from my prior employer that I noticed I was initially assigned $712,000 of budgeted accounts. By successfully cultivating relationships and proactively meeting the needs of my clients, I was able to grow those accounts to more than $1.79M in business, with nine of the accounts more than doubling in revenue!

Talk about underestimating your impact!

It's important to know and be able to acknowledge and verbalize what you have achieved, because it will be your responsibility to effectively communicate that to future clients, employers or other individuals. But you will be hard-pressed to do so successfully if you've never taken the time to explore what you have achieved and asked yourself why you were able to achieve that feat when others may not have done so.

What did I enjoy doing most/ What did I least enjoy?

When thinking about this question, I urge you not to become overly politically correct. Oftentimes, people try to put a positive spin on their feelings and sentiments towards the jobs and experiences they have had, almost as if they're in an interview and I'm going to run back and tell the employer what they said.

It is great to place a positive spin on situations if you're in an interview; however, when you're trying to grasp the full idea of the things you would like to do and not do professionally, I would advise you not to sugarcoat anything with yourself!

This is *your* list! No one else has to see this information nor will this information be privy to employers while you are interviewing for opportunities (unless you choose to disclose your responses). In the event that you choose to disclose any of the information that you learn about yourself, I would suggest making sure you learn how to most effectively articulate your points, because you definitely do not want to come across as a negative person. For the things that you don't want to do, you should ensure that those responsibilities are not a requirement within the role for which you're applying.

During this process, it's imperative that you're honest with yourself. Do not worry about saying something you *think* others would *want* to hear you say or disappointing someone else... This part is all about you! That's why you're working on this individually.

Fortunately, throughout my professional tenure, I have been blessed in that I have not had any jobs I did not enjoy or jobs in which I dreaded going to work. But while I have loved all of my jobs, there were tasks within those jobs that I would have preferred to have completed by someone else or tasks that I found difficulty in completing.

When I worked for the staffing agency, while I loved having an opportunity to interact with the clients and job candidates, I often found it difficult acquiring the time to perform basic data entry—a necessary task to add candidates to our database.

Data entry was one of the least desirable tasks I was required to complete. I often found myself staying at the office for an extra hour or two past closing time to input my candidates into the database just so that I could keep up.

Just because I did not like doing data entry does not mean I didn't like my job. Now, you do the same... what were the things you disliked most about each of your jobs?

The answer should not always be "there wasn't anything I didn't like"- especially in the event that you're no longer employed at that company- because you're no longer there for some reason.

Is there anything I know I don't want to do—whether now or in the future?

I cannot reiterate the importance of being completely honest with yourself—and YES, I feel the need to reiterate this over and over again. You cannot identify the things you are most passionate about nor the things that will make you happy in your career until you take the time to truly learn about yourself.

In meeting with individual candidates, there have been so many times I talked to people about their jobs, likes, and dislikes and then when I asked what they were looking for, they would say something that directly aligned with what they said they did **not** want to do.

The conversation would sound something like this:

Me: So, tell me about the things you did not like about your job...

Client: I could not stand looking at numbers all day; I thought it was mundane and I didn't have much of an opportunity to actually talk to people, which I really enjoy.

Me: Ok, well it's great to know what you do NOT want to do... so what type of position are you ideally looking for?

Client: Something in accounting.

Me: (After glaring at them with a blank stare and perhaps making some sarcastic sound with a facial expression to match, I would respond) But you JUST SAID that you did not want to look at numbers all day...

Client: Yeah, I don't. But it's ok, I'm used to it. The pay is good and it's what I know.

Do not continue looking for jobs and positions that you do not like. You will NOT be happy with that job and you will not be as effective in doing the best that you can do.

By staying in a job you do not like or a role you loathe, you're doing yourself, as well as the company, a disservice!

There is nothing worse than having people work in roles they do not like! Think about a negative experience you've had at a restaurant or a store in which a person appeared frustrated with his or her job. Could you tell that they did not like their job? YES, we can ALL see it and they typically perform in a manner that breeds contempt.

On the other hand, think about an experience you've had with someone who appeared to like their job. They were probably more positive and they were more than likely friendly to their customers, smiled and actually appeared to enjoy their job. They may have been more willing to go above and beyond to help as well.

How did each of those situations make you feel? What were your immediate thoughts about the individuals? I'm sure that these two situations brought up two completely contrasting experiences and memories.

Far too often people settle in their jobs and they settle in positions or places that they should no longer stay. Stop settling in your career because it generally affects every other aspect of your life and the people who suffer most are those closest to you.

Passionate Pursuit of Purpose

I'm sure you've heard the saying, "If you do something you love you'll never work another day!"

Well, that's not true! You will work, but you will enjoy what you do. You will be happier while doing it and will more than likely yield better results. But you *WILL* work.

This leads me to this chapter's last direct question to you –what are you most passionate about? If you're not sure what that is, think about the thing that makes you the most animated, expressive, upset, frustrated, etc. What issues in the world today get you riled up?

What is your soapbox item? What is that thing that you would volunteer to do for free if you had all of the money and time in the world? What topic(s) do you most commonly complain about? What issues frustrate you?

As I previously mentioned, prior to starting Regional Consulting, I worked for a staffing agency, one of the largest locally-owned staffing companies in the Northern Virginia/ DC/ Maryland areas; which I absolutely LOVED!

After being directed spiritually to leave my job and approaching the end of the one-month notice period I'd provided to my employer, I was still unsure as to what my next step would be. That job was where I had gained the foundation of my recruiting experience- it was time to leave and I didn't have a plan.

In search of answers, I attended a "purpose boot camp"—which I had never previously heard of, but thought would assist me in finding direction.

At the one day event, Leah Payton said our purpose was the thing that we have been created to solve. We have been equipped since youth with a variety of resources and life experiences that will aid us in fulfilling our purpose.

She asked about the things I liked doing when I was young. She inquired:

What did you want to be when you were younger? What makes you angry/ upset? What are the things that come to you naturally or the things you do with ease that others may have to work at?

In beginning to explore these questions, I will be honest; I did not have a clue as to what I was purposed to do or how to answer any of the above questions. But on my drive home, I immediately began thinking about all of the candidates I would voluntarily consult with to provide training and consultative advice prior to their interviews. I would help tweak small areas and empower them to be more successful in their interviews. Many of the individuals that I coached went on to successfully obtain positions.

I was also reminded of a specific gentleman who had come in to interview as a referral from a corporate client. The young man did not make a positive first or second impression during the interview. Not only was he unprofessionally dressed, but he chewed gum and even answered his cell phone during the interview! ALL of which are ABSOLUTE No-No's!

After telling my manager about the situation and being told to "do what you feel is best," I was prompted in my spirit to help him. I brought him back into the office to provide coaching on how to interview, gave him tips on how his dress can determine success, I rewrote his resume and even coached him on how to keep a job. He later went on to get hired by one of our toughest clients who paid a hefty placement fee to hire him.

It's important to do what you love. Take time to explore exactly what that is and what it means for you. When you operate in your gift, you can't help but love what you do, but also become successful while doing it.

At the time, I did not know professional development training was a passion for me, nor did I ever think that it could turn into a career; however, nine years later, after having impacted thousands of people from middle and high school students to corporate professionals, I can say that I am truly walking in my purpose and I ABSOLUTELY LOVE what I do!

Chapter Recap

We covered tons of information in this chapter! If you have not taken the time to write down your jobs, list your responsibilities for each job, explain what you have achieved, establish what you enjoyed and what you didn't from each position... PLEASE do not move on from this chapter!

It is imperative to your entire search that you complete this process and I implore you to really take time to examine and evaluate your past experiences because it can be instrumental in creating your future path to success.

Now that you have completed this chapter, you should have:

✓ Detailed all of your professional experience over the past 10-15 years
✓ Identified the things you liked and disliked about each of your jobs, achievements and contributions in each of your positions
✓ Determined your passions

HALFTIME:
DETERMINING YOUR
STRATEGY
(Just For Students)

If you're a high school or college student, you may feel that you don't have significant work experience to offer a potential employer.

THAT IS NOT TRUE!!!!

This chapter is designed specifically for students, whether in high school, college or soon-to-be college graduates. Here you'll find insight on what you can do now to boost opportunities both academically as well as professionally.

In the event that you are not a student, feel free to skip this chapter. Although if you are someone who is transitioning to a completely different industry or profession, start reading at the *Identifying Experience* section found later in this chapter. It will be beneficial to you as well.

Why this chapter?

When I was in high school as well as college, I could only WISH that someone would have given me the insight and training on interviewing skills, resume writing as well as other topics of professional development that I provide to students through my company, Regional Consulting.

I made so many mistakes along the way. I could have benefited greatly from someone advising me about what activities and opportunities would be most beneficial for my career. I did not have a clue about things that I should have been doing at various points in my life—some things I did because I enjoyed doing them; others were things that I "fell into." I later learned the value of those activities.

When I graduated from college, one of my biggest frustrations was finding a job posting that seemed perfect for me, but then reading on and discovering the most hated phrase for me at that time- "minimum 3 years' experience required." I graduated from Appalachian State University and during my collegiate experience I did not have an opportunity to work as an intern, so I found myself at an impasse.

My desire is that this chapter will not only help students, like you, with identifying things that will be beneficial in your academic and professional lives, but also to address some of the most common thoughts and ideas that can hinder future pursuits.

Thinking back to my high school and college experiences, I remember wishing that time would hurry and go by faster so that I could graduate and move on with my life. I remember thinking I was too young to do anything that really mattered and I wondered what my future would look like.

I didn't know, and no one shared with me, that the things you do in high school and college help determine the future opportunities you will have access to later on. You may already know that your academic grades will help determine your access to opportunities after high school, such as getting accepted into college and obtaining scholarships. But another neglected and overlooked asset can be your level of involvement in school and with outside organizations. You can use this involvement on your resume to demonstrate that it helped you build character and obtain invaluable experience.

I want to prepare you for your future by ensuring that you have valuable information to put on your resume, as well as on those college or career applications.

Before I go further with this section, let me help those of you who do not think that you're smart enough to go to college. Not only do I empathize with you, I thought the same thing until I was an aide in my high school counseling department and was forced to develop relationships with the counselors.

Mrs. Dillard was the counselor who sat me down and asked me which colleges I had applied to and she inquired about my plans after high school. I had previously been avoiding the counseling department altogether because I was afraid that question would arise. When she inquired, I responded honestly and I told her, "I'm not smart enough to go to college."

When I thought about college, I thought college students were much like *Doogie Howser* (a dramedy from my pre-teen years that featured Neil Patrick Harris as a teenage doctor) as well as students on "A Different World." I thought college students were all geniuses and that I was not intelligent enough to make the cut. Rather than deal with the possible rejection, I chose not to apply instead.

It was at this time that Mrs. Dillard put me in check using her sharp verbal abilities. After our conversation, I had a natural curiosity and began applying to colleges and to my astonishment; I was accepted into every college to which I applied.

With that said, wherever you are in your high school career, make a commitment to work harder and actually apply yourself. You too can get accepted into college. If you're already in your senior year of high school and you have not done well in school, it is still not too late. You can apply yourself the remainder of the school year and go to community college for a year or two, and then apply to the colleges or universities of your choice.

Knowing what I know now, I would have done so many things differently in both high school and college. Lucky for you, you get to benefit from the lessons I learned the hard way.

Get a Better Understanding

Now, I want you to consider a few possible career paths you would like to take when you graduate.

Whether you're in high school or college, after deciding on a few career paths, try to identify individuals or professionals who are doing what you think you would like to do. If you're in high school, you can reach out to your guidance counselors and ask if they can refer you to someone in your chosen profession. You can also ask your parents or older siblings if they have any recommendations of individuals you can speak to. When you mention to your parents that you are contemplating possible career options, trust me, they will be excited you have begun thinking about your future and they will do everything they can to help you in this process.

Make sure that when you ask any of the aforementioned individuals for recommendations that you are specific about what you're looking for.

The reason you want to be specific is because it's like asking a friend, "Where would you like to eat?" The most common response is typically, *"I don't care. I don't have a taste for anything."* Then when you say, "Ok, I was thinking hotdogs, hamburgers or Mexican. Which would you prefer?" they respond, "I don't have a taste for any of that, but I now have a craving for some Hibachi."

It works the same way with people. If you ask a question that is too general, it is easy to blank out and forget possible connections. If you ask your teacher or counselor, "Do you know any doctors?" they may be hard-pressed to think about an actual doctor just off the top of their head. But if you ask, "Do you know any pediatricians or an OB-GYN," it may be easier for them to think of either their own specialized doctor, friend or a neighbor in their network.

For college students, I would also recommend that you reach out to your Career Development Department and/or academic advisors. YES, your college more than likely has one! You can also reach out to your professors as well to discuss potential contacts— especially those that are in departments that align with specific industries. I would recommend having this conversation as early as possible–do not wait until your senior year!

In the event that you have not been able to start taking courses in your major, which is common for many freshmen and sophomores, you can introduce yourself to one of the deans within the department and ask for referrals or get to know one of the professors, because often times, they may have either worked directly in that industry or know of someone who has done so. You can also put those unused office hours professors set aside for students to good use.

Additionally, for college students, LinkedIn is also a great resource for finding professionals within specific hard-to-find industries. LinkedIn is one of the BEST ways to connect and network with industry professionals and also find job opportunities. You can search LinkedIn using industry as well as geographic preferences.

Once you identify individuals that are in the industry you're looking to go into, send them a connection request that will identify who you are and why you would like to connect with them. Do NOT send the generic email that LinkedIn prompts, which says "I'd like to connect with you on LinkedIn." You will want to say something like:

> *Good afternoon Mr. Smith. I am a (year in school) at (name of college) and I came across your profile while looking for individuals in (name of industry). I would love to connect with you to learn more about your profession as a potential career.*

Please note that there is a character limit on connection emails, but you can customize it or shorten it as necessary, such as abbreviating your school name, or saying "Hello" versus "Good afternoon" or you can say "I'm" versus "I am" Make sure that the abbreviations that you use are common knowledge, but are not considered what I like to call "textese"- such as TTYL.

One of the greatest potential resources can be to search for alumni of your university who are doing what you want to do.

If the person has an email address listed, you can also send an introduction email which details who you are, as well as why you're looking to connect, prior to sending the LinkedIn request, so that they are expecting your connection request. Make sure that within the introduction email that you mention coming across their LinkedIn profile, as well as the fact that you will be sending them a connection request to keep in touch or follow-up.

Also, make sure that when you reach out to professionals that you check your grammar, spelling and for simple mistakes because you want to come across as someone who is serious about their career.

Another thing I would like to mention to you is the need to remain professional with your contacts. Sometimes people may be really easy to talk to and seem like they're really nice to just hang out with or feel compelled to share a lot about yourself; but please exercise caution when taking professional relationships to your personal life. You never know whether a person that you connect to will become a future boss and it's best to exercise caution and professionalism.

With that said, please be aware that there is a chance some people you reach out to may not respond to you. Do not take this personally or send them derogatory messages asking why they didn't respond. People are busy, emails get lost in the shuffle. Some people do not check their LinkedIn accounts regularly. Just move on. There are many people in the field who you can reach out to and would potentially love to help students find their way.

When you receive a favorable response and have a chance to speak with the referral or connection, have a candid conversation with your chosen professional about their career path. You will want to take notes on the conversation as well. Some of the questions you can ask include, but are not limited to:

o What are the things you like and don't like about your career?

o How is your work/ life balance?

o What is an average starting salary in your industry and geographic location?

o Knowing what you know now, what would you do differently?

o What advice would you give to a student looking to pursue your career?

In the event that you are able to develop a good rapport and relationship with the individual, you may also want to ask if you can possibly shadow them or visit the work site so that you can see the type of environment for yourself. Sometimes students feel resolute on pursuing a particular career until they have the opportunity to obtain first-hand experience and they gain a more comprehensive understanding of the day-to-day reality of the job.

Make sure that at the end of the conversation or interaction with the professional, you let the person know that you truly appreciate the time they took in speaking with you. You may also want to send them a handwritten thank you letter to their job—you should be able to find their company's address online. This will show them your appreciation as well as the fact that you valued their time.

I advise seeking a better understanding because when I went to college, I was convinced that I would become an athletic trainer. I am what I consider to be a "footballnista" (a woman who is an avid football fan and watches almost every NFL game weekly and may actively participate in several fantasy football leagues—I typically play in at least 3 leagues each season) and I wanted to work on the sidelines for an NFL team.

When I finally began looking at colleges, I would only consider schools that specifically had athletic training programs because I did not want to study kinesiology or sports medicine, despite the fact that they're similar; I wanted to be an athletic trainer. Fast forward to the end of my sophomore/ beginning of my junior year when I FINALLY had the chance to work with our football team.

From the first day I walked into the training room in the Field House, I was smacked with the realization that the pungent aromas in the locker room merged with my newly-realized foot phobia would thwart my impending career plans and forever change my career trajectory!

For Aspiring Professional Athletes

Speaking of sports, I'm sure there are students who think that they will have a career as a professional athlete and will never have to apply the information in this book. Let's remember and acknowledge that there is a life after being a professional athlete. Tyrone Smith, a friend of mine who is an ex-professional NFL player, once told a group of students at one of the high schools that I speak, that the NFL stands for "Not For Long!"

According to the NFL Players Association, the average tenure of a professional football player is 3.3 years. A basketball players' average career is 4.8 years, according to Business Insider. So even if you are one of the chosen few to play professional sports you would likely retire by the age of 28 or 30. So, what happens next for those who are not lucky enough to be a Darrell Green, Jerome Bettis, Adrian Peterson or Tom Brady?

Well, I'll help you with that answer. Many athletes start a second career in hopes of continuing to provide for their families. I've had a few ex-athletes reach out to me to help them seeking assistance with writing resumes for their new ventures. Others ride the sports ride as long as they can, hoping to start a career as a sportscaster, which can be extremely competitive and requires the ability to effectively articulate your value and what you can do as well.

I'm sharing this with you because I want you to recognize that your athletic talent is a resource that you can utilize to help you create your life after college or sports—whichever comes first. It is important for you to think about activities that you partake in outside of your sport because they will help define your future opportunities.

What does this have to do with resumes? I'm trying to emphasize the important fact that the actions that you take today CAN and WILL impact your future opportunities and your actions will determine whether you will have access to an abundance of opportunities or "nah."

Creating your Playbook

Every playbook began as blank pages.

I implore you to start creating the canvas and determining how your future will look NOW!!!

1. First, determine what you want to do and **create a path** to get there. "If you don't know where you're going, any road can get you there." — Lewis Carroll.

One of the reasons many people are not successful in life is because they settle for the mediocrity that was presented to them at some point in their lives. They never set goals or decided to strive for more. They feel like they are exactly where they should stay in life. "Why fix what is not broken?" they say and they can't imagine life getting better. But I assure you that it can!

2. Determine what you are most afraid of or the thing that will keep you from successfully completing your goals. Les Brown, who is a prolific motivational speaker, said *"Most people fail in life* not because they aim too high and miss, but *because they aim too low and hit."*

Much of the reason I think most people aim low is because they are afraid of failure or being told "No." I challenge you today to identify the things that may immobilize you from doing what you desire to do. Understand that you will make mistakes in life, they are inevitable. But learn to use your mistakes as learning opportunities and not something that will hinder you from moving forward.

I dare you to be bold and post your goals on Instagram or Twitter and tag me **@RegionalConsult** and use the hashtag **#BoldlyPursuing**. I want to hear about what you're inspired to do.

Sometimes the hardest part is convincing yourself that you are able. I want you to put it in writing. It's not real until you see it in writing and are reminded of it every time you see it. You can also find an accountability partner to hold you accountable on your path to success. This person should be someone you trust and will celebrate your victories and will help you fight through your fears, tears and the hard times.

I encourage you to **strive for more** and continue to break through barriers and to metaphorically kick down doors you may have otherwise been afraid to knock on! You have so much greatness inside of you and can achieve insurmountable things if you just keep going. Do not get sidetracked by fear or failures.

3. Commit to being a well-rounded student. Maintain good grades and also become actively involved in a sport, club, organization or activity you enjoy or an activity that is closely aligned with your career goals.

When I was in high school and even college, one of the things I enjoyed most about going to school were my after school activities and organizational affiliations. I ran track and was also President of the Spirit Club and 1st Vice-President of Student Council. I was active in the Spanish Club, DECA and also served as President of ICC (the club that oversaw all school affiliated organizations) while in high school.

In all sincerity, I think it was likely the breadth of my extracurricular activities that helped me to get into the various colleges for which I applied, because I maintained good grades while also demonstrating a heavy involvement in school- helping me to distinguish myself as a well-rounded student.

While in college, I was also active in various organizations—

Black Student Association (BSA), Ladies Elite Service Organization, Council for Cultural Awareness (CCA) and the Spanish Club.

I will be honest and note that some of my organizational involvement in college was because the organizations offered free food! But, it doesn't matter what got you there–the important thing is - you WERE there!

Being actively involved in extracurricular activities helps you develop character and intangible skills that can easily translate into a variety of fields. It also supplies you with information you can easily utilize to demonstrate your contributions on your resume.

4. You should also **start volunteering or get a summer job** for organizations that are aligned with your area of interest. If you want to be a veterinarian, you should volunteer to work at the humane society or a pet shelter. Perhaps you may want to obtain a position at a zoo, pet store, pet grooming salon or somewhere you can get hands-on experience working with animals. If you're an entrepreneur at heart, you can also start your own pet care or walking service as well.

Volunteering is one of the best ways to obtain industry-specific experience that allows you direct insight into what that job will entail. Imagine wanting to be a veterinarian and finding that after you've worked so hard to complete school; you're scared or allergic to the pets you want to work with. Some things you can only learn through direct experience and volunteering is a great way to help narrow things down.

5. **Find and utilize your available resources** at your school. Getting to know your guidance and career counselors can be extremely invaluable to your future.

As I mentioned to you earlier, one of my high school guidance counselors was instrumental in encouraging me to apply for college, because she saw potential in me I was unable to see in myself. Counselors are also extremely knowledgeable about scholarships, internships and opportunities that may go unnoticed by those who aren't involved.

Despite the fact that my guidance counselor in high school was pivotal in helping me to get to college, I did not realize the value of communicating with the academic advisor about more than my credit hours while I was in college.

She could have informed me that we had a separate Career Development department that would not only help me write resumes and search for jobs, but would also schedule me for interviews with employers who visited the campus.

I did not realize that I had this resource at my disposal until the second semester of my senior year when I passed a friend walking down the street who was headed to her final interview for a major company. I learned that day that the company had previously visited the campus on several occasions throughout the semester to interview and recruit students and to my dismay, they were recruiting in the area of Public Relations, my chosen field of study. I was so disappointed with myself for missing out on those opportunities– but I can't complain too much because I LOVE where I am today!

It is my hope that you will learn from my growing pains. Find and use all of the resources available to you. Be cognizant of the playbook you're creating on that blank canvas.

Identifying your Experience

Although the information from Chapter 2 definitely applies to students, it is the expertise gained from your organizational involvement and extracurricular activities that we will utilize to construct resumes for students and soon-to-be graduates (who do not possess hands-on work experience).

In the event that you have not completed any internships and do not have actual job-related experience; you may utilize the information we discuss below to build your resume.

Your content can consist of activities you've been involved with, ranging from various membership organizations and clubs to class and group projects you've worked on. This is one of the reasons why it is imperative for you to become actively engaged in your school, community, volunteerism and/or other organizations.

Often times, we take for granted our role in the planning processes and do not consider how the actions we have previously taken and the roles we have played can directly relate to our career aspirations.

Here are some questions you may want to ask yourself to jog your memory of the experience you've gained as a student:

o   What class or team projects have I worked on?
o   How many people were on my team?
o   What were the end results?
o   Were we commended or recognized for our actions or project?
o   Did we start any new trends, traditions or student-led activities?
o   Are there numbers I can quantify that resulted from our class project? (How many people were in attendance, how much money was raised, how many people did we

directly or indirectly impact, how many people did we serve, etc.?)

o What was my role within the scope of the project from creation of the idea to the project's completion?

o What challenges did you face and how was a resolution determined?

o What was your role in the problem-resolution process?

o Did this activity set any precedents for the class/organization? For example, will others be expected to do the same thing in the future or was there a lesson learned that will be applied going forward?

o Who coordinated the meetings and planned around everyone's schedule?

o How did you determine where the meetings would be held and how was the meeting space obtained? Who obtained approval for the use of the facility?

o Were you responsible for obtaining sponsors or vendors?

o Were you directly involved in negotiation of any activities or special rates?

o How many people and what level were the individuals you coordinated with on your teams and for your project?

Your list may be a few pages and it's great if it is! It's better to have too much information and have the opportunity to narrow it down than not having enough detail.

Here is an example of experience you can document that will be beneficial in customizing your resume:

While in one of my public relations classes at Appalachian State University, my class was tasked with completing hypothetical group projects that would allow us to present a mock proposal, where our teams would promote growth and improve the image of an already existing organization.

Our team was comprised of about five or six people who, much like myself, were all very competitive and accustomed to exceeding expectations within their endeavors.

We partnered with our client, Love Me 2 Times, which was a vintage clothing store and a local non-profit organization called Watauga Youth Network (WYN), which provided mentoring to youth.

Rather than simply doing the task that was assigned by our professor as a hypothetical, we took our project further and went above and beyond the required assignment. Our group chose to host a fashion show that would allow us to not only promote Love Me 2 Times; but it also gave us a chance to introduce WYN and their efforts during intermission to everyone in attendance.

Additionally, we secured a bar where we would host the entire event, which helped bring customers to the bar and they were able to promote their specials to attendees; as we chose a bar that was not as commonly frequented by students.

The night of the fashion show, we had more than 100 people in attendance in the tightly packed space (in fact, so many people were in attendance that some people had to sit on the stage) and we also raised several hundred dollars that we were able to donate to WYN to assist in their efforts. We were also successful in promoting the clothing of Love Me 2 Times, as we modeled their clothing in the fashion show and we acknowledged them as a sponsor.

Here's a picture of my modeling debut... AND FINALE!!!

For students that may have organizational involvement, here is another example. I was also very active within a number of organizations during my undergraduate experience, such as Ladies Elite, a service organization dedicated to aiding Watauga County and promoting sisterhood.

While involved with Ladies Elite, all active members contributed to planning and coordination of activities, service projects, fundraisers among other events hosted by the organization. My tasks ranged from contacting organizations and solidifying dates for activities to reaching out to organizations to obtain sponsorship for events.

I'm sure that if you're a student reading this book right now, you may be thinking... that reminds me of this project I worked on for an organization I'm a member of... STOP NOW and write down all of the information and details you just remembered! This will all become extremely important in the next chapter.

If you're a recent or soon to be college graduate, you should try to obtain as much experience as you can within your desired field of interest through internships, co-ops, volunteer opportunities, etc.

Today, focus on writing down what you've already done and also continue identifying areas that can potentially help you in your future professional aspirations.

Chapter Recap

This chapter was devoted to helping break through restrictive mindsets that can hinder students from achieving their educational and professional pursuits. We discussed a variety of tips that can help shape and prepare students for their future, the importance of gaining insider knowledge on desired career industries and we identified things students can do to create their path to success.

Now that you have read this chapter you should have:

✓ Spoken with your guidance, career counselor, teacher or parent about identifying individuals in your desired profession and reach out to them to speak further

✓ Pinpointed the fears that are possibly preventing you from achieving your goals

✓ Determined academic experience that can transfer over to your career

✓ Thought about and determined how you want your playbook to look in the future and start working towards accomplishing those goals

✓ Identified academic or organizational experience that could be utilized in creating your resume

3RD QUARTER STRATEGY: ANALYZING YOUR STRATEGY

Identifying What You Want

Now that you have finished compiling your comprehensive list of experience, you should take the time to really think about what you want to do. Start by identifying the types of positions which align with your personality and find companies and jobs that align with your desires. In this chapter, I will also teach you how to decipher a job description.

If you are confident in your career path and know exactly what you want to do, feel free to skip over this first section and go to the section entitled "Deciphering Values and Job Descriptions," later in this chapter. However, if you have even the slightest fragment of doubt about your career path or if you do not truly like what you do, please continue reading this section.

What type of positions truly interests you? Take the time to actually identify specific positions that align with your area of interest and expertise. Keep in mind that there are not any companies recruiting for a position called "anything"— therefore, that's not a possibility. You must be more specific.

Just because you have a specific area of interest, does not necessarily mean that it is an area that you should pursue professionally.

For example, while I mentioned being a huge NFL fan and passionate about football earlier, I am NOT going to team practices or the NFL combine to put on pads and act as if I'm auditioning for teams. I highly doubt any team would secure me as the wide receiver or safety that I am (at least in my mind)!

There are also going to be professions where you will need to obtain experience, certification, training, etc. to obtain an actual role in that field. You will not be able to rely solely on transferrable experience for all roles.

Your areas of interest should be realistic and something you are qualified for and can possess or obtain relevant experience.

In the second chapter, you identified the things you liked and disliked about the various roles in which you have previously been employed. This is where many of those things will come into play.

Evaluate the things you said you liked doing as well as the things you disliked. Now that you have a better understanding of the things you enjoy and do not enjoy, it is important that you begin to pursue careers that align with your individual interests.

A few questions you may want to ask yourself include:

- Am I happy in my job? If not, do I really want to do something about it?
- Are the things I previously listed as enjoyable within my role, prominent responsibilities in my industry, profession or role?
- What types of positions require doing the things I enjoy doing most?
- Are the things I disliked doing prominent responsibilities in the role for which I am applying? If so, how much time will be dedicated to doing that (or those) task(s)? Can I be successful if a large portion of my job requires this individual responsibility?
- Is it more important for me to be happy or pursue a new job in the same area I began my career?
- What type of company do I want to work for?
- What is most important to me at this current time in my life?

If you're still not sure what you would like to do, you may also want to take one of the many online personality assessments that can help you identify best careers for you based on your personality type. Some of these assessments can be found online for free. Go to your preferred search engine and type in "free career assessment" and choose a test.

Tests can last anywhere from 5-10 minutes, such as the Career Perfect Work Planning Inventory, E-Learning Planner or Coach Compass Hemisphere's assessment, while others may be more time intensive, such as the Kiersey Temperament Sorter and Testing Room Personality Index.

Please note that while the resources I mentioned are currently offered for free, some of the organizations offer more detailed reports for an additional cost. There are also additional assessments that may have costs associated with them. Feel free to explore as your financial resources allow.

One of the books I highly recommend for professionals from any industry sector is Tom Roth's *StengthsFinders*. The StrengthsFinders assessment helps you identify your top five strengths and it also tells you how to best operate within your strengths. Make sure that, if you purchase the book, do not buy a used version, as there is an access code that you will need to enter in order to take the online assessment.

Should you decide to take the Strengths Finders assessment, you can also do a reverse career search by googling careers that align with the areas of your top five.

The thought that this is a very intense process may be crossing your mind at this time. I will admit it definitely is; however, think about it... some people spend just as much time, if not more, working than they do sleeping at night. So the time you put into researching your career will pay off in the end and will hopefully contribute to a better quality of life.

While contemplating your search, I would also implore you to think about the areas you are most passionate and have excelled the most within your career. What are some of the things you do well without even trying?

You must determine what your priorities are at this time in your life. Priorities change over time, so you need to re-evaluate them every few years or when major shifts occur in your life. Priorities will vary for different people. The most important priority for me right now is making an impact with regards to professional development for high school and college students, as well as corporate employees that will help them live happier, more purpose-filled lives and will allow them to elevate their professional lives.

I have a good friend who is waiting for her daughter to graduate from high school next year before she makes any career changes. The quality time she is able to spend with her family is her most important priority and brings her the most satisfaction at this current time.

It's important to gauge these things because as an individual who is able to passionately pursue and walk in my purpose, I can tell you that there is nothing more fulfilling! Besides, what is the point in going to a job you loathe? If your professional job is clashing with your roles in other important aspects of your life, you are not going to be content.

So many people wake up on Monday morning wishing they could have one more day for the weekend and wishing they did not have to go to their job.

There is a HUGE difference between "having" to go to work and "*getting*" to go to work.

I implore you to choose the latter, it's definitely worth it!!

Deciphering Values

Now that you have taken the career assessments and have a better idea of the type of position you're seeking, let's delve into researching companies and positions that align with your goals, objectives and desires.

Since you have identified your essential priorities, you need to search for companies that have the same or at least similar values. Ask yourself, what are the things that are most important to me? Make a list of those things so that you can hold yourself accountable later in your search. Once you determine your greatest values or the things you believe in most, you can begin to assess companies for their values.

Does the company value work-life balance? Do they value green energy? Does the company value their employees? How does this company feel about the changing environmental factors and is that a big deal to you? Are you looking for a company that values community service or social responsibility? Feel free to add your questions.

Whatever a company values will be at the forefront of everything they do.

A great example of this model, whether you agree with their values or not, is Chick-Fil-A. When the company was started, they began the company with strong Christian values and *all* of their franchisees must adhere to their rules and regulations. Most notably, *all* of their restaurants are closed on Sunday. That is a nonnegotiable for the organization. They are also service driven. Have you ever noticed that anytime you tell one of their employees "Thank you" they respond by saying "My pleasure"?

The service level expectation is also prevalent in their store activities and in the way that they address problems. I once received the wrong sandwich for breakfast and after driving back to the store, they provided me with a replacement sandwich *and* refunded me the purchase price for my inconvenience. Chick-Fil-A lives by its company values.

You should also begin to review job descriptions for roles that align with your targeted profession. First, you should look for all job titles that captivate your interest. Then you should search for actual positions within the companies that align with your desired objectives. This is a task that can be completed using online search engines, a variety of large job boards, such as CareerBuilder, Glassdoor, Indeed and The Ladders, as well as LinkedIn and other smaller or industry-specific job boards.

Once you have identified a number of jobs that appeal to you from your ideal companies and positions, narrow the list down to the top 3. In your ranking, take into account all details that are available to you (location, salary range, experience required, etc.).

Decoding Job Descriptions

After identifying the top 3 positions, select the most appealing position to you. Then print the job description and read the description again. This time, highlight the most important duties, experience and responsibilities that have been emphasized throughout the listing.

When reviewing job descriptions, have you ever noticed that there are typically a few common themes that are repeated and stated in different ways? That is one of the ways to distinguish the most crucial requirements—look for redundancies in the description.

You can also tell the essential requirements and non-negotiable factors by the things the job listings state as "must haves." For example: Candidate must possess a minimum of 5-7 years' experience working with XYZ software.

Chances are, if a job listing says that you **must** have a minimum of "X" number of years and you do not meet the minimum requirement within the specified area that was mentioned or closely relatable experience, you will not be considered for the position. First and foremost, applicant tracking systems want to know: *Does this candidate meet the basic requirements for the position?*

Using a different color, also highlight the qualifications that are mentioned as pluses. Example: "PHR, SPHR certification a plus."

In the margins, wherever space allows, write the top 5-10 most crucial overall requirements that a candidate must possess for that specific position.

In re-reading the description one last time, use a pen and underline the experience you possess which aligns with what the employer is asking for within the description. This would be a good time to review the notes you took on Day 2 that contains all of your experience. This is the reason I had you detail as much as you could possibly remember.

Let's take a look at a sample job description so that we can walk through how to implement the information that we just discussed.

This position was provided courtesy of one of my client organizations, NightLight Pediatrics, which is a phenomenal and rapidly growing urgent care after hour's clinic for children in Texas. I was provided authorization to use a prior job description for which I previously provided recruiting assistance. Please note that a few areas within the job description have been modified for more generality.

I underlined the important and relevant requirements, extra qualifications they desired; double underlined when I found a match with my skills and experience and used bold lines for things that were pluses.

Job Summary

Seeking <u>Full-Time Recruiter</u> with <u>3-5 years' experience overseeing the full lifecycle recruitment process</u>. The recruiter will <u>partner with managers</u> within Nightlight Pediatrics to <u>anticipate and meet the evolving staffing needs of the organization</u>. The recruiter will be responsible for <u>hiring strong candidates</u> in a <u>variety of medical positions</u>.

We are <u>currently in expansion mode</u> and <u>hiring and employee management responsibilities may extend beyond Houston</u>.

Job Duties

- Assist with <u>recruitment and selection processes for both back and front-office hires</u> for positions ranging from <u>front desk</u> & medical assistant to pediatricians & nurse practitioners
- Conduct <u>phone and face to face interviews</u>
- <u>Prepare and implement recruiting strategy</u>
- Provide <u>guidance & partner with managers to determine job specs and candidate requirements</u>
- Perform <u>background & reference checks</u> for preferred candidates
- <u>Plan and conduct new employee orientation</u> to <u>foster positive attitudes</u> for organizational objectives
- <u>Conduct exit interviews</u> with departing employees and <u>provide analysis of feedback</u>
- Complete special projects by <u>clarifying project objectives, setting timetables and schedules, conducting research, development and organizing information, fulfilling transactions and assisting with implementation of organizational objectives</u>

- o Maintain employee HR records (new hire forms, promotions, performance reviews, etc.)
- o Administer employee development, training programs and employee education programs
- o Use social and professional networking sites and other cost effective recruiting strategies to identify and source top talent
- o Other tasks as assigned

Requirements

- o Requires Bachelor's Degree
- o 3-5 years of professional human resource and recruiting experience
- o Prefer professional HR certification such as PHR, SPHR
- o Excellent computer skills, including experience with MS Office, Word, Excel and Access
- o Excellent communication skills, both verbal and written. Must be able to interact professionally and positively with employees of all levels of the organization

Candidate must have knowledge of general HR best practices and trends; ability to work independently and exercise good judgment; capable of managing highly confidential information. Healthcare experience is a plus, but is not required.

The person for this job will have to be a self-starter, creative and efficient with their time. Most of all, they need to be a people person, confident and committed to excellence.

Despite all the vast experience and requirements listed in the job description, you can summarize the entire position by a few main concepts:

o   Effectively communicating with various audiences
o   Maintaining confidential information
o   Serving as a business partner and retaining relationships with constituents on all levels
o   Performing tasks that are considered to be "due diligence" and "best practices" in recruiting (screening resumes, phone and in-person interviews, on-boarding of job candidates, reference checks, etc.)

You will likely find similar trends within the positions you are applying for as well.

Therefore, when writing your resume, you will want to focus on the information that helps sell your experience that is most relevant to the position for which you are applying. You should also make it most relatable to the potential employer. I'll share more on that later.

In the event that you see terms such as: due-diligence, best practices or other terms that may be unfamiliar, you should research those terms so that you can identify the meaning and their significance for your industry or position. Due diligence in recruiting will be different than the tasks you would complete as due diligence in accounting.

Researching the terms will help you gain insight on the expectations for the position.

Lastly, identifying the hierarchy of responsibility and highlighting within the job description is a process you should complete for each position which you apply for going forward, because your resume should be tailored to meet the organizations' needs. There is not a "one-size-fits-all" resume.

I am aware this is a very time-consuming process and will require you to sit down and process the information and complete tasks you are not accustomed to doing when looking for a job. You're right! That is one of the reasons I do not recommend being a "serial applicant" to any specific company or position.

A serial applicant is someone who applies for positions almost any time they see available positions posted and despite their experience, they consistently apply to company or job listings.

As someone who has recruited extensively, I can attest to the fact that when candidates repeatedly apply for positions (especially positions for which they are not qualified), recruiters begin to start recognizing names. Just as with anything that is overused, recruiters can become desensitized to your resume. You want to avoid recruiters getting to the point where they may inadvertently ignore or avoid your resume.

Going through this process will help you become more strategic about the positions you actually take the time to apply for, because the process will not be as easy as a "Click to apply" for you any longer.

Chapter Recap

Although this chapter was much shorter in the number of pages, it was packed with information. We discussed the importance of identifying companies that align with your values and desires, performing career and personality assessments as well as deciphering job descriptions. Much of the information you gain while exploring these areas will become the crux of your resume.

Now that you have finished reading this chapter, you should have:

✓ A good understanding of the things you value and are looking for in a potential employer
✓ Performed a career or personality assessment to determine the roles that suit you best
✓ Determined the type companies you are most interested
✓ Narrowed your job search down to one specific position for which you will customize your resume in the next chapter

4TH QUARTER STRATEGY: POSITIONING YOURSELF TO WIN

Let's Make Things Clear

Jimmy Graham is a tight end in the NFL, who stunned everyone during his sophomore season when he emerged as a key offensive weapon in 2011. In fact, I've drafted him almost every year on at least one of my fantasy leagues since his sophomore season, although I failed to acquire him this season.

But Graham is an anomaly in the NFL, as he only played one year of college football; he was predominately a basketball player. The New Orleans Saints saw value in drafting a reasonably inexperienced college football player because they could see the *transferrable qualities* he possessed. His extreme athleticism, size and speed allowed him to make a tremendous impact for his former team because his vertical reach allowed him to catch passes that were otherwise uncatchable.

I'm sure you've seen me use it previously, but it's a term I want you to know and become very well acquainted: transferrable experience. It's one of the most important aspects in the customization of your resume.

As I stated earlier, job seekers have a tendency to provide, what I consider to be, a complete regurgitation of their experience from every position they have had. They leave it up to the potential employer or recruiter to determine why they're a fit for the position which they're applying.

Simply put, transferable experience is being able to communicate why what you have done is relevant to the position you're applying for even though it may be in a completely different environment, industry or profession.

For example, if the only experience I have is working in a fast food restaurant, but I was responsible for answering phones and taking drive-thru orders; I may not have experience functioning as a receptionist, but my experience is relevant because I can define how what I have done allows me to contribute to the new position.

As a job seeker, it is YOUR responsibility to identify the experience that makes you a good fit for the position which you are applying. *You* must translate the relevance of the experience you possess within your resume so that the person responsible for hiring can understand why he/she should give you a shot at an interview and potentially hire you.

It's important that you customize your resume for each type of job you apply for as well. For example, if you're interested and qualified for HR positions in recruiting as well as training & development, then you should have a customized resume for each of those specific areas, especially in the event that you must upload them to job boards.

Why is it necessary to create multiple resumes? The car buying process is a great comparison to a job or career search.

Would you ever walk into a car dealership and say: "I want to buy a black vehicle"? Being vague about what you're looking for in a position or failing to tailor your resume to the specific position is as ridiculous as shopping for a black car with no regard to year, make, model, body style or cost.

The first thing the salesperson is going to do is ask you a series of questions to identify how they can best assist you, qualify you and determine the type of vehicles they should and should not show you.

Some of the questions the salesperson would likely ask:

o   What type of vehicle are you looking to purchase?
o   Are you interested in a sedan, coupe, minivan, SUV, sports car, etc.?
o   How much are you looking to spend?
o   Do you have your own financing or will we be assisting you with that today?

If you need to be specific when you're purchasing a car, which depreciates in value as soon as you drive it off the lot, why would you feel you can be any less specific about a job where you will potentially spend a large part of your day and 40+ hours a week?

You may remember that in chapter 2, I helped you understand the difficult choices that recruiters must make on a daily basis in order to fill positions. During this process, don't forget how important it is to assist the recruiter in seeing your value! You do not want to have the recruiter confused as to why you are the best candidate. They will simply move on to another resume.

By failing to tailor your experience, you are doing yourself a huge disservice and you're selling yourself short!

Answering your objections

You may be thinking that spelling out your relevance to a potential employer is a waste of time. *Most jobs are self-explanatory,* you may say.

> *If a person has been a receptionist at one company, then you pretty much know what is expected for every other receptionist, right? I shouldn't have to be specific about how my experience matches the job posting.*

WRONG again!!

Let me explain it to you like this: Even though I am not a car enthusiast, I can generally tell distinct cars apart. My youngest nephew, David on the other hand, is extremely passionate about cars. One of his favorite cars right now is the Dodge Challenger SRT Hellcat. He constantly talks about all of the features and amenities as well as its exceptional speed and performance, despite the fact that he isn't even old enough to drive and he's never been behind the wheel of a car.

When I look at the Hellcat and compare it to the regular Dodge Challenger, they both look fairly similar to me and I can't truly distinguish which car is the Hellcat or the regular Challenger. However, by looking at the subtleties, my nephew can immediatly identify the car correctly from hundreds of feet away.

Let me put it another way: Can you tell the difference between a McDonald's Chicken Sandwich and a Chick-Fil-A Chicken Sandwich?

I've had the opportunity to train different audiences ranging from middle and high school students to corporate executives and when I ask whether they can tell the difference between the sandwiches, respondents from all ages and socio economic status often reply with a resounding YES!!!

The first response and most overwhelming response I receive is that they can tell the difference because of the quality. Many of the individuals who have had both of the sandwiches can quickly distinguish one company's sandwich from the other—not only aesthetically, but also through taste and smell.

If it's easy for us to distinguish one company's product from its competitor, how much more do you think a company knows the qualities and experience they're seeking within the candidates for their available positions?

One of the things you will get to learn by gaining experience within different organizations is that not all positions have been created equally at all companies.

In the example above with receptionists, in some companies, a receptionist's responsibility may only be to answer phones and transfer calls. Other companies may require that the receptionist also greet visitors, perform light clerical responsibilities and also maintain calendars and schedules of executives and conference rooms.

Meeting the requirements

Next, you should identify companies as well as job descriptions that align with your desires. Look for postings that will allow you to apply your transferrable experience while at the same time ensuring that you meet all of the necessary educational and professional requirements. There is no point in looking at Senior Engineering positions when you know you have never been an engineer.

Similarly, having the mindset that you're looking for *any* job will get you nowhere fast. As we've discussed in previous chapters, you must learn what YOU want to do and become more strategic in navigating your professional career.

Getting back to the car example, saying that you're looking for "anything" would be the equivalent of going into a car dealership and telling the salesperson that you want a car that has tires, doors and a steering wheel. ALL cars are equipped with those things, but narrowing your search down to a sports car that has a V-6 Engine with push-button start and leather interior may eliminate a lot of vehicles (even though it still doesn't completely confine the search). But the more specific you are, the more easily you can narrow your search.

I can't tell you how many times I have received resumes from job candidates that have worked for a few years as receptionists but have applied for senior level engineering or management positions. Why? Because they did not take the time to thoroughly read the job description and what the employer was seeking beforehand. In addition, they have not taken the time to identify what they are skilled to do in order to make an informed choice regarding positions for which they should be applying.

Sometimes, though, they have taken their skills and experience into consideration and they have applied for jobs for which they do not qualify. My question is: *Why are you wasting your time?*

If you know you're looking for a sports car, why waste your time looking in the minivan section?

Seeking out and applying for positions that are relevant to your goals is extremely important.

Identifying Transferrable Experience (Students)

Now that you have identified the position you would like to apply for, you will want to look at your previous experience and ask yourself: *What have I done that is most relevant to the tasks related to this role?*

Also ask yourself, *how will I communicate this experience to the employer so they can understand that my experience is relevant to this position?*

I will utilize the job description for the Recruiter position, which I provided in chapter 3, to show you how this can be done.

Please note that students should only apply for entry-level positions, or positions that require no more than three years' experience if they are fresh out of college and do not possess any professional experience.

A few of the requirements listed in the description is the need to work with staff on all levels of the organization, conducting candidate phone screens and interviews, serving as a business partner as well as training and development.

o Assist with recruitment and selection processes for both back and front-office hires for positions ranging from

front desk & medical assistant to pediatricians & nurse
practitioners
o Conduct phone and face to face interviews
o Prepare and implement recruiting strategy
o Provide guidance & partner with managers to determine
job specs and candidate requirements

Because in Chapter 3 you took a complete inventory of your
collegiate tenure, this should be an easy task. The following examples
will demonstrate how to translate experience you may have gained
from group projects, organizations and seemingly unrelated
experiences into relevance for a job position.

A little earlier, I mentioned to you that while I was in college, I
worked on a major project where my group hosted a fashion show to
promote the organizations we previously discussed.

In order to determine which organizations we would partner
with, as a group, we came together to decide on our project goals;
then it was up to us to find organizations that met those goals. It was
also our responsibility to introduce ourselves to the organizations,
build relationships with the clients and we also had discussions with
the business partners to make sure our goals meshed well with those
of the organizations. I was thoroughly involved with all aspects of the
planning and strategy development process.

During my collegiate experience I also mentioned my
involvement with Ladies Elite service organization. Prior to joining
the organization, I was aware of two of the largest events that were
hosted annually by the organization–The Mr. Elite pageant as well
as Showtime at the APP-ollo; which also happened to be two of the
largest fundraisers for the organization as well.

Mr. Elite pageant was a male version of a beauty pageant in which male participants competed to win the crown in various areas, inclusive of modeling and talent. The men were appraised by official judges and upon completion of the event, a new Mr. Elite would be crowned and he would work on various projects throughout the year to help serve in collaboration with the organization.

"Showtime at the APP-ollo" was our version of the show "Showtime at the Apollo" in which contestants competed by promoting their talent of choice. We also permitted random acts that garnered "boo's" and would be met with "The Sandman" who would usher the act off stage.

Upon becoming a member, we were tasked with all responsibilities in relation to the planning, coordination, promotion, participant selection, as well as other areas for the events. It was also our responsibility to secure the location and dates for the event. Our members met bi-monthly to discuss other organizational goals, events and ideas to promote the organization and we also helped with identifying ladies that could potentially serve as future members.

While in college, I also had several jobs as a restaurant hostess at various restaurants. Within my longest tenured position, not only was I the hostess **supervisor**, but I was also responsible for:

o   making desserts
o   training new hires
o   ensuring we had the necessary dessert inventory in stock
o   overseeing the staff in my department
o   providing managers with feedback on employee performance

One of the processes I started with the hostess staff was during peak operating times and after double or triple seating a server, I trained the host staff to immediately take the drink orders from the customers to provide to the server. The hostess would obtain the soft drinks and give alcohol orders to the server. This helped to make sure the customers did not have to wait long to receive service–which drastically improved our customer experience and helped ease wait staff during peak times.

These are all skills and experience that can be included in a resume that go beyond what some might think a restaurant hostess does. It's your job to connect the requirements listed in a job posting and translate the relevance of your experience.

Identifying Transferrable Experience (Professionals)

If I were to look from a professional experience perspective, I would perform the same tasks I asked you to do earlier and write down all of the tasks I performed within my positions. I will provide a little of the most pertinent insight most relevant to the Recruiter position that was previously posted.

My experience working at the staffing agency afforded me many opportunities to gain my footing in the area of recruiting and human resources.

I was responsible for a variety of tasks from building relationships with clients, following up with clients to solidify job descriptions and training new associates on job duties to interviewing candidates, placing candidates within positions that aligned with their abilities and negotiating pay and bill rates for job candidates and businesses.

Within our office, as a team of four recruiters (at most), we managed anywhere from 140-190 active job listings. We were also tasked with staying in touch with our clients to provide them with updates on our progress in hopes of retaining their business and patience throughout the process.

Choose your words wisely

Previously, when I discussed keywords, I mentioned you should avoid throwing in random keywords in hopes that the computer software or resume reviewer will grant you access to a real-life person. However, that does not mean you should not use keywords at all.

Utilize your keywords strategically and ensure that they have a purpose and that they demonstrate what you have done in that specific area within your expertise.

Look at the list of what you have done and what you have achieved and compare those things to the job description you identified as the position that most closely aligns with your interest. (You should already have a list of things you achieved from that long list you created in chapter 2 and/or 3).

From a recruiting perspective, bullet points typically work best because they are short and quick snippets. You're not holding the recruiter "hostage" by making them read long paragraphs.

In the event that you are transitioning industries or going into a new area and you're not familiar with the keywords that are most pertinent to the industry for which you're applying; it's up to you to become knowledgeable of the industry lingo. Go online and do a google search on your industry as well as the terms related to it.

Notice the words the employers use within the job descriptions as well as the words they use interchangeably.

One of the other things you should strive to do when recounting your experience on your resume is make tasks action-oriented, which means, don't just tell me what you have done, tell me the actions you took to achieve the task. Also tell me what you achieved or explain the significance of a task.

That is the reason I had you list as much detail earlier on the things you were able to accomplish in your positions. It is so much easier when you have this information at your disposal and can utilize it where it is most applicable.

Honesty matters

We are almost to the point where we can put all of the hard work that you have done throughout your tasks into motion.

But before we get started, let me tell you that this is not the time to try and downplay your experience, contributions or to be too humble about the actions you have taken. You don't want to downplay your experience, but you also don't want to make it more than it was. Just be honest about what you have done and what you were able to achieve.

It's important not to overly exaggerate your experience, abilities or accomplishments. If you sell the fact that you have done something very well or have experience in a particular area, and then you cannot perform those tasks without direction, training or coaching after you are hired—"HOUSTON, we may have a problem!"

Additionally, the company may be unwilling to provide you with the necessary training, when they may have been willing to do so if you hadn't stretched the truth or misled them regarding your experience level.

Lastly, you must think about your references. If the employer contacts your references, will they be able to vouch that you were responsible for these tasks and have the skills you claim to have on your resume?

There is nothing worse for a recruiter than going through the interviewing process, thinking you've found the perfect candidate, obtaining the client's approval and then when it's time to extend the offer, speak with a reference who contradicts what the candidate said or what's on the resume. It's like walking hundreds of miles in the desert only to find that the oasis you thought was within reach was only a mirage.

Chapter Recap

We discussed several pivotal areas within this chapter that will be instrumental in creating your resume and will best demonstrate your value- transferrable experience, the importance of using keywords that align with the hiring company's desires as well as how to identify transferrable experience from both a student and a professional perspective.

Now that you have finished reading this chapter, you should have:

✓ Compiled a complete list of transferrable experience that is relevant to the specific position in which you're interested
✓ Identified the keywords and requirements for the position you identified in Chapter 4
✓ Defined any industry terms that you may be unfamiliar

OVERTIME STRATEGY: FINISHING STRONG

Pulling it All Together

We are almost in the final stretch of the process!

Now that we're almost to the end, let's look at how we can put all of the hard work you have done into one resume that genuinely promotes your experience and makes employers want to call you.

Whether you're a student or an experienced professional, the first thing you should do when actually starting to write your resume is review the job description again to get a full understanding of the key qualifications that the company is seeking and the best skills you can offer.

The best way to start this process is to start by looking at the job summary again:

Seeking Full-time Recruiter with 3-5 years' experience overseeing the full lifecycle recruitment process. The recruiter will partner with managers within NightLight Pediatrics to anticipate and meet the evolving staffing needs of the organization. The recruiter will be responsible for hiring strong candidates in a variety of medical positions.

We are currently in expansion mode and hiring and employee management may extend beyond Houston.

The Objective Debate

Depending on who you ask, you'll receive a different answer about whether or not you should include an objective statement on your resume. If your objective says something like: "seeking a position that will use my experience" then you probably should NOT use an objective.

A clear objective sets the tone for the resume that will follow because it is naturally the first thing recruiters see when they open your resume. I always say that the test of a good objective is if you can isolate the objective statement from the rest of the resume and still know exactly what that person is seeking as well as what they can offer.

Here is a sample objective statement for the recruiter position:

Seeking a Recruiter position that will effectually merge more than five years full lifecycle recruiting and strategic HR experience with impeccable communication skills and ability to function as a tactical business partner assessing company culture, business and talent needs, while aligning HR solutions to maximize future growth within a healthcare organization dedicated to exceptional care and superior services

That statement is fully loaded and may be overwhelming for some, but notice that it defines many of the things I want the employer to detect first and foremost. You can condense some of the information should you feel the need, however, I was strategic about formulating the objective.

Notice that within that statement, I chose what I identified as the top three qualifications the employer is seeking for the position, which also aligns with the experience that I previously identified within my expertise.

I would also like for you to notice that I ended the objective with information that is specific to the organization for which I would be applying which, in this case, is NightLight Pediatrics. That was done so that I can show the employer that I am not looking for just ANY position and that my resume has been customized specifically to their position.

Make sure you actually research the company or organization to ensure that your resume reflects the company's values.

In order to continue writing the remainder of the resume, you will have to determine the information you want to present about yourself and what would make you stand out most.

In looking at the above job summary, the main duties are to: oversee the full life-cycle recruiting process, partner with managers and anticipate the needs of the organization.

With an understanding of the job summary, go back to the job description where you identified the most pertinent experience the company is seeking for this position (which we identified earlier), so that we can stay focused on the position.

- o Communicating with different audiences
- o Maintaining confidential information
- o Serving as a business partner and retaining relationships with constituents on all levels
- o Performing tasks that are considered to be "due diligence" and best practices in recruiting (screening resumes, phone and in-person interviews, on-boarding of job candidates, reference checks, etc.)

Customizing Bullets- Student Perspective

Looking at a similar entry-level position from a student perspective, you can easily apply the relevant experience from the group projects, student organization and hostess position to fit the requirements for this job.

By highlighting the experience that best aligns with organizational needs, my Objective would read:

Seeking a Recruiting position that will merge impeccable communication skills, exceptional employee management and leadership capabilities with innate ability to function as a strategic business partner while identifying best possible solutions within a growing medical company that values exceptional service and superseding expectations

In detailing my experience, I would likely create bullet points that pull all of the things we previously discussed together. A few of the points I would want to highlight are:

- o Collaborated with 5 seniors to research, identify and select organizations that closely aligned with PR project requirements, which resulted in a successful fashion show raising $500 in a one night student-attended event to contribute to organizational support of local non-profit organization

o Established mutually beneficial partnerships with owner of vintage clothing store, Love Me 2 Times and WYN, a local non-profit organization to promote awareness of previously unrecognized mentoring organization and recognition of unique apparel company, resulting in drastically increased foot traffic and augmented student support

o Trained newly hired employees on job responsibilities, processes and procedures to ensure superior operational performance and encourage repeat business

o Implemented new systems and processes for hostess staff, designed to proactively address customer needs while simultaneously providing exceptional customer experience

o Confidentially evaluated employee performance and provided detailed assessments to senior managers to provide updates on front-house operational staff

o Contributed to optimized overall organizational performance by suggesting departmental enhancements

These are just a few of the points I would make, but you may notice that each of the points are related to one of the aforementioned goals. I also added a dimension of training as well as the ability to analyze organizational needs in as well, as the body of the position mentioned training as a responsibility.

When I was an undergraduate, I was not aware that I should track my success by recording tangible results- even from my classes.

But fortunately, you have an advantage over me because you can start today. Keep track of all the details of your achievements both now and in the future.

Hind sight being 20/20, I would have tracked more closely how much foot traffic the organization had before and after the event so that I could more precisely recollect the direct impact our project had for the company (increased by an average of 30 customers per hour). I would have also obtained the exact donation amount we were able to contribute to the organization as well as the headcount of people who were present.

Customizing Bullets- Professionals Perspective

As a seasoned recruiter, I have a more definitive set of accomplishments. Looking back on old performance reviews, I was able to create a customized, detailed, quantifiable list of my direct impact:

- o More than doubled revenue in nine accounts, earning profits of more than $1.79 million dollars of a projected 712K budget within one year of assuming account management responsibilities by cultivating more strategic and mutually beneficial partnerships with hiring managers at client sites
- o Consistently recognized as recruiter with most placements, averaged 170+ placements quarterly
- o Selected as sole recruiter for new two-person startup office and partnered with manager to surpass yearly goal of $1M within eight months
- o Sourced, recruited and placed almost 100 candidates at a rapidly-growing client site in less than a 2-year period

with less than 10% turnover while working an average of 20-25 hours weekly

o   Assisted clients with local, national and global recruiting services and sourced for opportunities ranging from Sales/Operation Managers to Engineers, C-level and other technical and niche positions

o   Maintained open lines of communication with clients to build relationships, confidence and establish trust within struggling accounts to salvage partnerships, often resulted in improved client relationships

Notice that all of the things I mentioned within the individual bullet points were directly related to the experience that NightLight is seeking for their new employee.

As you've seen, this book does not focus largely on the design and layout of the resume—my purpose was to get you thinking about the importance of the content within your resume.

With that said, I have created two versions of the resume for this position—one is for the entry-level candidate that is a recent college graduate and the other for the more seasoned professional. I narrowed the resume down to the most pertinent skills and experience.

Recent Graduate

Juanita Hines

M: (555) 756-7465   209 Appalachian Dr., Boone, NC 28607   jhines@fakeemail.com

Objective

Seeking a Recruiting position that will merge impeccable communication skills, exceptional employee management and leadership capabilities with innate ability to function as a strategic business partner while identifying best possible solutions, within a growing medical company that values exceptional service and superseding expectations

Summary of Qualifications

- ✓ Effectual communicator, experienced conversing and tailoring communication with various levels on the employment spectrum from subordinates to colleagues and organizational leaders
- ✓ Proven leader, capable of effectively managing and leading employees while obtaining best results
- ✓ Strategic thinker and resolute decision maker accustomed to conceptualizing and implementing successful and creative results-oriented solutions designed to meet departmental needs
- ✓ Exemplary time management skills, best utilized in fast-paced, deadline-driven environment
- ✓ Technically savvy individual, proficient with MS Office Suite and capable of learning proprietary systems with ease

Education

Appalachian State University   08/2012- 05/2015
Bachelors of Science in Communication- Public Relations, minor in Spanish   Boone, NC

Work Experience

Popular Student Restaurant   05/2013- 05/2015
Hostess Supervisor   Boone, NC
- ➢ Trained newly hired employees and directly supervised up to 8 on job responsibilities, processes and departmental procedures to ensure exceptional operational performance and repeat business
- ➢ Confidentially and discreetly evaluated employee performances and provided detailed assessments to apprise senior managers on front-house staff execution of job responsibilities
- ➢ Contributed to optimized organizational performance by suggesting departmental enhancements
- ➢ Utilized stringent task prioritization, leadership and time management skills to determine most urgent departmental priorities and delegated tasks to garner most positive overall impact
- ➢ Implemented innovative process for hostess staff, designed to proactively address customer needs while simultaneously easing wait staff angst during peak hours, resulted in exceptional customer relations and decreased wait times

Additional Experience

Class Based Projects   08/2014- 05/2015
- ➢ Collaborated with 5 seniors to research, identify and select organizations that closely aligned with PR project requirements, which resulted in successful fashion show raising $500 in a one night student-attended event to contribute to organizational support of local non-profit organization
- ➢ Established mutually beneficial partnerships with owner of vintage clothing store, Love Me 2 Times and WYN, a local non-profit organization to promote awareness of previously unrecognized mentoring organization and recognition of unique apparel company, resulted in 45% more customers, increased foot traffic for apparel store and augmented student support of non-profit

Ladies Elite Service Organization   04/2012- 05/2015
Treasurer, Parliamentarian and General Member   Boone, NC
- ➢ Identified, solicited and recruited contestants for male pageant and talent show contests to attract heightened student participation and augmented attendance of more than 120 people
- ➢ Communicated and maintained relationships with organization and departmental leaders to provide updates on follow-ups and collaborated with partnering organizations on joint-effort projects

Experienced Professional

Juanita Hines

M: (555) 826-7426   432 For Real St, Fresno, TX 77545   juanitah@fakeemail.com

OBJECTIVE

Seeking a Recruiter position that will effectually merge over five years full life-cycle recruiting and strategic human resources experience with impeccable communication skills and ability to function as a tactical business partner assessing company culture, business and talent needs while aligning HR solutions to maximize future growth within a healthcare organization dedicated to exceptional care and superior service

SUMMARY OF QUALIFICATIONS

✓ Efficacious communicator, adept interacting with all levels of the employment spectrum and tailoring communications towards targeted audiences, ranging from entry-level to C-suite executives
✓ Adaptive training and recruiting skills, capable of strategically aligning resources with key practices
✓ Technically savvy individual, proficient using MS Office and learning proprietary systems with ease

PROFESSIONAL EXPERIENCE

Regional Consulting   **04/2012- Present**
Contract Recruiter   Houston, TX
➤ Sourced, recruited and placed almost 100 candidates at a rapidly-growing client site in less than 2 year period with less than 10% turnover while working an average of 20-25 hours weekly
➤ Utilized guerilla recruiting techniques, resulted in savings of $5000 to 25,000 in annual subscriptions
➤ Periodically reviewed agency contracts and renegotiated bill rates to decrease overhead and diminish unnecessary expenses, saving clients an average of $5000 to 10,000 for each candidate placed
➤ Spearheaded local, national and global recruiting services and sourced for a variety of positions ranging from Sales/Operation Managers and Engineers to C-suite, technical and niche positions
HR Business Partner
➤ Maintained open lines of communication with clients to cultivate more robust relationships, confidence and rapport while aiding clients with salvaging deteriorating partnerships and restoring trust
➤ Trained clients on how to effectively screen candidate resumes for job opportunities and evaluated candidate skillsets to source best candidates for available opportunities aligned with company culture

Staffing Services   **06/2010- 04/2012**
Senior Staffing Supervisor   Washington, DC
➤ More than doubled revenue in nine accounts, earning profits of more than $1.79 million dollars on 712K projected budget within one year of assuming account management responsibilities by cultivating more strategic and mutually beneficial partnerships with hiring managers at client sites
➤ Consistently recognized as recruiter with most placements, averaged 170+ placements quarterly
➤ Preserved extremely confidential information on daily basis, which ranged from personal employee information, performance evaluations and counseling sessions to employee pay and client bill rates
➤ Selected as sole recruiter for new two-person startup office and partnered with manager to surpass yearly goal of $1M within eight months
➤ Performed full life-cycle recruiting services for client openings while proactively managing, cultivating strategic relationships and overseeing the growth of 10-20 accounts
➤ Recruited for various Fortune 500, non-profits, government contracting as well as for-profit companies including, but not limited to: Booz/Allen/Hamilton, KPMG, BearingPoint, ADA, SHRM, CSC, UNCF, etc. for a variety of office support, customer service, professional and technical positions
➤ Trained new in-house employees on duties, responsibilities as well as expectations and provided performance evaluations and feedback to senior management
➤ Maintained open lines of communication with clients to build relationships, confidence and establish trust within struggling accounts to salvage partnerships, often resulted in quadrupled revenue

EDUCATION

Appalachian State University   **05/2010**
Bachelor of Science in Communications with a concentration in Public Relations, minor in Spanish

Resume Formats

While I will not take a lot of time to go into the different types of resume formats; I will provide you with a quick overview on the types of resumes.

There are three basic types of resumes: chronological, functional and hybrid resumes.

Chronological resumes focus on time, hence the "chrono" prefix. Within chronological resumes, you list your experience starting with the most recent experience first and then go backwards. These types of resumes are best utilized to demonstrate good job stability and work history that is relevant to the next position for which you are applying.

Functional resumes highlight the skills and talents that candidates possess which are closely related to the position they're applying. This format typically helps increase the chances for those who may otherwise look weak when listing their experience using a chronological format. This style is generally utilized when people are transitioning to a new type of position or when they want to take the focus off of their job stability. Functional resumes focus on the function, rather than the time.

Finally, the hybrid resume is a mixture of both the chronological resume and the functional resume. This style emphasizes good work history, job stability as well as relevant experience.

We utilized the hybrid resume in our sample resumes.

As I previously mentioned, there is a ton of information available on formatting, design and layouts for resumes; however, that is not the focus of this book.

Three Questions

Now that you have had an opportunity to review the resume samples, you are almost finished. There are just a few final tasks you should complete before calling your work of art complete and submitting it for review.

You must now go through the resume and ask yourself three questions for each piece of information listed on your resume.

The three questions that you will want to ask yourself are:

o   What did I do?
o   What did I achieve?
o   If I do not list this experience on my resume, will the lack of having this experience cost me this job opportunity?

The key in evaluating your responses and answering these three questions is not adding or taking anything away from what you have written on the computer or paper.

When we are familiar with the subject matter (in this case, you are intimately familiar with your work history) we have a tendency to add additional insight as we read. We fill in the blanks and understand much more than the words that are written. Remember that the employer will NOT be privy to the information in your head.

We use lines to justify, such as: "they will know what I mean"; "everyone does this (fill in the blank)" or "it's close enough." This is why you need to read what you SEE not what you INTENDED to say or convey!

The importance of going back to review each bullet point is almost as essential as deciding which points to emphasize!

Let's look at an example:

o   Sourced, recruited and placed almost 100 candidates at a rapidly-growing client site in less than   2 year period with less than 10% turnover while working an average of 20-25 hours weekly

What does this experience say I did?

It says that I was responsible for all aspects of the recruitment process for a client that was growing quickly. Did NightLight mention anything about growth within their job description? Yes they did! They mentioned that they are in the expansion process.

What was I able to achieve while carrying out this task?

This bullet demonstrates that on a part-time schedule, I was just as effective as someone who is a full-time recruiter. Even if we were to look at the fact that I only worked part-time, I was able to successfully place almost 100 candidates, which averages out to hiring almost 1 person per week! Imagine what I could do in a fulltime capacity!

I also stated that the turnover was less than 10%, which says, not only can I recruit people expeditiously, but I can also hire the right people that align with the company culture and performance standards.

If I neglected to list this information on my resume, would it likely cost me the opportunity?

I think that failing to list this experience would definitely be detrimental for me because it affirms the fact that I am able to recruit the right people, quickly and in abundance—three key elements to success in this position.

Let's Take a Walk

Before finishing this chapter, I wanted to take an opportunity to walk you through a few things I did within the resumes.

Objective

I like good and firm objectives, as they set the tone for your resume and tell the employer what you really want as well as what you can offer. I focused on the skills and experience that I possessed as a student or as a seasoned professional and they highlighted why I would be a great candidate.

If the recruiter stopped reading at that point, I think they would definitely be interested in at least speaking further—which is, once again, the purpose of a resume! If you think the objective is too wordy, you have the option to make it shorter; however, my purpose was to put it out there to capture the recruiter's attention.

You may have also noticed that there are not any periods used within the objective statement, as well as the resume for that matter. The reason you do not need periods is because periods are used for complete sentences. The sentences that you will construct within your resume are not complete because they lack a subject (I, me, my, etc.). Subjects should never be used within resumes and you should also avoid writing resumes in the third person (Suzie is great at…).

With that said, some people choose to use periods at the end of their incomplete sentences, but whether you choose to use them or not, make sure that you stay consistent throughout the entire resume because that will be an indication of your attention to detail for employers.

Summary of Qualifications

The Summary of Qualifications (SOQ) is not a requirement for resumes; however, I tend to use them within majority of the resumes I have written. The purpose of the SOQ is to highlight the most important elements of an individual's experience first. As you will notice, the seasoned resume had fewer bullets than that of the recent graduate.

The reason I did this is because, as a recent college graduate, I would likely not have specifically done all of the required tasks within the job description, but, if I possess specific qualities that lend themselves to the position, I can at least demonstrate why I should be given a chance to speak further about my potential.

Within the SOQ, you want to highlight the top skillsets you possess which align with the requirements the company is seeking. For each category on the resume, you have a greater chance of having the information skipped over if by scanning the resume, the recruiter assumes that you do not possess the experience they're seeking.

Additionally, I chose to list the summary prior to the education because I did not want the recruiter to stop reading and assume that just because a person is a recent graduate, he/she does not have any relevant experience. Don't get me wrong, not all recruiters will, but I've talked to quite a number of them who have and will do so. Just as a rule of thumb, if you do not have any official experience, you should not apply for any roles requiring senior-level experience.

Within the SOQ, I listed the skills in order of importance in accordance with the skills I identified as most important from the job posting. I based this ranking on repetition within the job description and significance to the position.

There is not a set number of bullet points for this section, although I generally try to use no more than eight and no less than three at a bare minimum. If you only need one or two, you can usually list them under the professional or specified work experience.

Education

As a recent graduate or someone who has successfully obtained a degree within the past five years, your Education section should precede your professional experience.

If you graduated more than five years ago, your education should go at the bottom of your resume. There are some positions that differ, such as positions in education and a few other industries, but this is a general rule of thumb.

You may have noticed that I did not list GPA or Dean's List information. This was simply for spacing purposes because the resume would have likely spilled over onto two pages. If you use a second page, I recommend having enough information to fill the page rather than having a one and a half page or a quarter page resume.

If the position was listed for a recent college graduate and asked for specific qualifiers such as "time management while prioritizing," I would've likely said something about maintaining a specific GPA (3.0 or better) while serving as an active member within a variety of organizations.

In the event that your GPA was lower than 3.0, you may want to avoid listing it all together (unless the information is required or if you're using that information for a specific purpose, i.e. demonstrating character development, growth and maturity, etc.).

I've literally seen students highlighting the fact that their GPA was 2.3! I figured that they did not know they had an option to leave it off.

Work Experience/ Professional Experience

Many people tend to use the Work and Professional Experience headings interchangeably; however, I like to think of work experience as something that is not gained in a career oriented manner (qualities or experience gained in school or other ways that may not be directly related to the industry or position you are applying).

In my opinion, it is the difference between a job and a career. A job is something that you go to for the purpose of earning a paycheck; a career is where you plan to grow within your professional pursuits.

Additionally, within this portion of the resume for the seasoned professional, you may notice that I have chosen to separate the Business Partner from the Contractual Recruiting services. The reason I did that was because I wanted to focus on each individual aspect of the role and I also did not want to diminish the tasks completed within various portions of my experience.

This is also because I have my own company and have the ability to function in different capacities. If your job titles and responsibilities are the same or similar, you can simply focus on the most relevant experience first and rank each by hierarchy of importance.

You should consistently ask yourself, *what is the most important information I can share for this job?* Then list that experience first while asking, *what would happen if the recruiter stopped reading after this portion?*

If I was in Corporate America and wanted to highlight the fact that I was promoted quickly, rather than leaving the dead space on the ends, I would list out the dates for each of the positions and it would look something like:

Name of Corporate Company   04/2012–Present

Senior Recruiter   10*/2014–Present*

- o Promoted to senior recruiter within six months due to demonstrated leadership and ability to create successful strategic partnerships by identifying best personnel in correlation with organizational objectives

Recruiter   *04/2014–10/2014*

- o Additional information you want to highlight within this position

You may also notice that different numbers of bullets are used within each of the resumes and sections. Contrary to popular belief, every section on your resume is not required to have the same number of bullet points, nor is there a specific number of bullets you must use for each job listing.

As I'm sure you've noticed on the seasoned professional's resume, the experience within the staffing agency had more information that was valuable, which is the reason the position has more bullets.

I have heard the question asked on numerous occasions: what if all of my positions are similar? Should I just repeat the bullets?

Rather than repeating the same tasks under different positions or copying and pasting the information, you can divide the points you want to share within each of the roles and highlight different portions of your experience within each of the roles.

As I previously mentioned, each position does not have to detail exactly what you did, it only needs to describe what you did in relation to the position for which you are applying.

Lastly, notice that I quantified as much information as possible within the positions on each of the resumes.

I will mention that for the student resume version, I added or tried to best recall the direct figures as shared by our clients, although you may notice that it is not exactly what was provided within the previous experience I detailed earlier in the book. Much of this is due to the fact that this is a hypothetical resume in which I'm demonstrating how to include the information.

Additionally, this is one of the reasons you want to obtain as much detailed statistical or numerical information as you can while you're actually working in the position or in school. Students will have the benefit of reading this book prior to graduating, so you're already ahead of your competition.

If you attended college more than five years ago and you possess professional experience, you should not continue listing experience you gained from college on your resume. The purpose of utilizing information from college is to show that you were able to focus on your academics as well as extracurricular activities while managing your time effectively and being a good student— qualities that demonstrate your potential impact and can transfer to the professional world.

Formatting

The last thing that I would like to bring to your attention is the overall formatting of the resume. Notice how I am subtly directing your eyes to the direction I want you to read. All of the bullets are evenly aligned with each other. You can take a ruler and look down the right margins of the page from the start of the email address and it will be along the same line as the dates, cities and anything else that is listed on the right side of the resume.

Notice that what we did for one section of the resume, we also did for all the other sections. For example, look at the spacing between the headings. Each of them has only one line in between with the headings underlined. Also, note that if one of the dates was bolded on the resume, we bolded all of them that shared the same formatting.

To demonstrate that the aesthetic appearance is not the most important thing about the resumes, I reformatted the looks for each of the resumes in the next pages. Please note that the only thing that has changed is the visual appearance of the resumes.

Reformatted Recent Graduate

Juanita Hines

M: (555) 756-7465	209 Appalachian Dr., Boone, NC 28607	jhines@fakeemail.com

Objective

Seeking a Recruiting position that will merge impeccable communication skills, exceptional employee management and leadership capabilities with innate ability to function as a strategic business partner while identifying best possible solutions within a growing medical company that values exceptional service and superseding expectations

Summary of Qualifications

- ✓ Effectual communicator, experience conversing and tailoring communication with various levels on the employment spectrum from subordinates to colleagues and organizational leaders
- ✓ Proven leader, capable of effectively managing and leading employees while obtaining best results
- ✓ Strategic thinker and resolute decision maker accustomed to conceptualizing and implementing successful and creative results-oriented solutions designed to meet departmental needs
- ✓ Exemplary time management skills, best utilized in fast-paced, deadline-driven environment
- ✓ Technically savvy individual, proficient with MS Office Suite and capable of learning proprietary systems with ease

Education

Appalachian State University   08/2012- 05/2015
Bachelors of Science in Communication- Public Relations, minor in Spanish   Boone, NC

Work Experience

Popular Student Restaurant   05/2013- 05/2015
Hostess Supervisor   Boone, NC

- ➤ Trained newly hired employees and directly supervised up to 8 on job responsibilities, processes and departmental procedures to ensure exceptional operational performance and repeat business
- ➤ Confidentially and discreetly evaluated employee performances and provided detailed assessments to apprise senior managers on front-house staff execution of job responsibilities
- ➤ Contributed to optimized organizational performance by suggesting departmental enhancements
- ➤ Utilized stringent task prioritization, leadership and time management skills to determine most urgent departmental priorities and delegated tasks to garner most positive overall impact
- ➤ Implemented innovative process for hostess staff, designed to proactively address customer needs while simultaneously easing wait staff angst during peak hours, resulted in exceptional customer relations and decreased wait times

Additional Experience

- ➤ Collaborated with 5 seniors to research, identify and select organizations that closely aligned with PR project requirements, which resulted in successful fashion show raising $500 in a one night student-attended event to contribute to organizational support of local non-profit organization
- ➤ Established mutually beneficial partnerships with owner of vintage clothing store, Love Me 2 Times and WYN, a local non-profit organization to promote awareness of previously unrecognized mentoring organization and recognition of unique apparel company, resulted in 45% more customers, increased foot traffic for apparel store and augmented student support of non-profit

Ladies Elite Service Organization   04/2012- 05/2015
Treasurer, Parliamentarian and General Member   Boone, NC

- ➤ Identified, solicited and recruited contestants for male pageant and talent show contests that attracted heightened student participation and augmented attendance to more than 120 people
- ➤ Communicated and maintained relationships with organization and departmental leaders to provide updates on follow-ups and collaborated with partnering organizations on joint-project efforts

Reformatted Experienced Professional

Juanita Hines

M: (555) 826-7426	432 For Real St, Fresno, TX 77545	juanitah@fakeemail.com

Objective

Seeking a Recruiter position that will effectually merge over five years full life-cycle recruiting and strategic human resources experience with impeccable communication skills and ability to function as a tactical business partner assessing company culture, business and talent needs while aligning HR solutions to maximize future growth within a healthcare organization dedicated to exceptional care and superior service

Summary of Qualifications

- ✓ Efficacious communicator, adept interacting with all levels of the employment spectrum and tailoring communications towards targeted audiences, ranging from entry-level to C-suite executives
- ✓ Adaptive training and recruiting skills, capable of strategically aligning resources with key practices
- ✓ Technically savvy individual, proficient using MS Office and learning proprietary systems with ease

Professional Experience

Regional Consulting   04/2012- Present
Contract Recruiter   Houston, TX
- ➤ Sourced, recruited and placed almost 100 candidates at a rapidly-growing client site in less than 2 year period with less than 10% turnover while working an average of 20-25 hours weekly
- ➤ Utilized guerilla recruiting techniques, resulted in savings of $5000 to 25,000 in annual subscriptions
- ➤ Periodically reviewed agency contracts and renegotiated bill rates to decrease overhead and diminish unnecessary expenses, saving clients an average of $5000 to 10,000 for each candidate placed
- ➤ Spearheaded local, national and global recruiting services and sourced for a variety of positions ranging from Sales/Operation Managers and Engineers to C-suite, technical and niche positions

HR Business Partner
- ➤ Maintained open lines of communication with clients to cultivate robust relationships, confidence and rapport while aiding clients with salvaging deteriorating partnerships and restoring trust
- ➤ Trained clients on how to effectively screen candidate resumes for job opportunities and evaluated candidate skillsets to source best candidates for available opportunities aligned with company culture

Staffing Services   06/2010- 04/2012
Senior Staffing Supervisor   Washington, DC
- ➤ More than doubled revenue in nine accounts, earning profits of more than $1.79 million dollars on 712K projected budget within one year of assuming account management responsibilities by cultivating more strategic and mutually beneficial partnerships with hiring managers at client sites
- ➤ Consistently recognized as recruiter with most placements, averaged 170+ placements quarterly
- ➤ Preserved extremely confidential information on daily basis, which ranged from personal employee information, performance evaluations and counseling sessions to employee pay and client bill rates
- ➤ Selected as sole recruiter for new two-person startup office and partnered with manager to surpass yearly goal of $1M within eight months
- ➤ Performed full life-cycle recruiting services for client openings while proactively managing, cultivating strategic relationships and overseeing the growth of 10-20 accounts
- ➤ Recruited for various Fortune 500, non-profits, government contracting as well as for-profit companies including, but not limited to: Booz/Allen/Hamilton, KPMG, BearingPoint, ADA, SHRM, CSC, UNCF, etc. for a variety of office support, customer service, professional and technical positions
- ➤ Trained new in-house employees on duties, responsibilities as well as expectations and provided performance evaluations and feedback to senior management
- ➤ Maintained open lines of communication with clients to build relationships, confidence and establish trust within struggling accounts to salvage partnerships, often resulted in quadrupled revenue

Education

Appalachian State University   05/2010
Bachelor of Science in Communications with a concentration in Public Relations, minor in Spanish

Do these individuals look any less qualified than the initial candidates based on content alone? No, of course not because the content has not changed.

Naturally, you will be attracted to specific versions of the resume, but the most important thing for you to remember is that the content is most important and it should be customized to the position you are applying.

It's not enough to have a good looking resume without the content to match. That's like seeing the man or woman of your dreams across the room only to find out that their inner beauty does NOT match their outer. I want you to be the total package for your future employer and I want to help you get in front of them so that you can have the opportunity to sell your experience and the value you would add to them!

Proofread, proofread, PROOFREAD

You've done the hardest part of the process! Congratulations, you're almost done! First, review the resume that you have customized for accuracy, content and clarification purposes while it is on your screen.

Formulate the resume until you believe you have produced the final draft of your resume.

Now, print out the resume you created so that you can see it on paper. The reason I want you to print it out is because it will help you identify the small things you may have missed in the electronic version.

Our minds are wired to figure things out and see things the way they are supposed to be. So when you are reading a document on the phone, tablet or computer, it's easy to skip over a misspelled word or tell yourself that you're going to go back and change something.

Have you ever sent a text message that you thought read perfectly clear only to see it again and notice you left out one of the main words that may have changed the context of the conversation. Perhaps it was the auto-correct feature that messed up your text—that's true, but it's still your responsibility to review it before sending.

This is the same reason I asked you to print out the job description as well.

Once you have finished proofreading your resume, you should have a friend or two look over the resume; but not just the resume, give them the job description as well so that they can help you identify whether the information seems to be relevant to the specific role.

Chapter Recap

We finally had the opportunity to put all of the pieces we previously discussed throughout this book together and you finished writing your first resume draft! We walked through the process of how to distinguish transferrable experience within your resume, making the resume action-oriented and customizing it towards the specific positions for which you are applying.

Now that you've finished reading this chapter, you should have:

✓ Completed the first draft of your resume implementing all of the points that were previously discussed

✓ Customized your resume towards the specific position you're looking to apply for

✓ Asked yourself the three questions to ensure the information contained within your resume is relevant and specific to the position you're applying for

✓ Proofread the digital version of your resume as well as a printed version of your resume to confirm accuracy, content and intention

✓ Identified a friend or two that you can ask to read the resume in conjunction with the job description

POST-GAME ANALYSIS: COACHING HUDDLE

First of all, allow me to congratulate you for making it through such a grueling, time-consuming and arduous process! In all honestly, I KNOW that this process has not been easy for you because I went through many of your same woes writing the book!

But you overcame your desire to quit (as did I) and I hope that you now have a great marketing tool that will highlight the relevant experience you have to offer to your next potential employer. Now the hard work will begin because you may need to identify additional positions you can apply for and perform this process over again to obtain your desired results.

I hope that completing this process will make you more selective about the positions you apply for and that you will be just as diligent about customizing your future resumes for opportunities because, as we previously discussed, there is not a one-size-fits-all resume. So let's make sure that you will not have to ask why you're not hearing back from employers anymore.

Before you finish, I have a question. What led to your desire to update your resume or read this book?

You may have been applying for positions and have not heard back from potential employers. Or perhaps you were recommended to read it by a friend. Or maybe you met me at one of my speaking engagements and took my advice to heart.

People oftentimes do not think about updating their resume until they are pushed to start looking for another job. That was my primary line of thought as well, until I provided my company with my resignation letter and quickly figured that I should update my resume. Despite my experience writing and customizing other people's resumes' as a recruiter, I too was stuck in the same place you were—frustrated about where to begin.

When people really enjoy their job and what they're doing; time passes extremely quickly and you look up and realize that you've been with the company for 5, 10, 15, 20 years and when asked what you've achieved, it's difficult to think beyond the most recent things you've done.

What if you wanted to apply for a position in another department in your company and they tell you that today is the last day they're accepting resumes? Or what if your employer suddenly had unexpected layoffs? Would you be prepared?

As you may have noticed while completing all of the due-diligence within this book, it is extremely easy to forget the things you have done within six months or a year—let alone five or ten years! If you make it a habit to keep your resume up-to-date, you won't be caught unprepared when an opportunity presents itself.

Let's say that you're a business owner, is a resume necessary for you as well? The answer is YES! Your resume can help you quickly sell your achievements to other companies or to future business partners as well because they can quickly identify the value-add you offer.

My recommendation is that you update your resume quarterly or at least bi-annually because you do not want to miss out on capturing the immense contributions you've made for your employer that could potentially be invaluable to a future company.

I would also recommend that you use the notebook you used to compile all of the requested information within this book for your resume as a job search notebook, so that you can easily track information on your job search. You can easily track your experience as well as other important details, such as the companies for which you have applied, dates, conversations with recruiters and more.

Keeping Track

If you've recently updated your resume, the steps in this book were likely much easier to complete than if you were starting from scratch or with old information. It is YOUR future and YOUR responsibility to strategically navigate your career, which is another book for another day!

For those who may not want to actually update your resume at least bi-annually, I would recommend that you maintain a running list of accomplishments saved on your computer that will contain all of the things you have recently achieved. Update this list at least quarterly with as much detail as you can track.

You can save the document as "Recent Accomplishments" and note the position title, dates, recognition, budget and any other quantifiable information you can obtain. It is much easier to obtain statistical data when you are employed with a company than after leaving–so it's better to have the information and not need it than to need it and not have it.

Make sure you also save the document somewhere other than your computer as well–perhaps in the cloud, on a flash drive or on an external hard drive, in the event that your computer crashes and you are unable to access the file (which is extremely frustrating and has happened to me).

As you mature within your career, you may have different desires—growing within your company, switching jobs/ companies, transitioning into an entirely different industry or perhaps starting your own company. Whatever route you choose can be more easily navigated by maintaining good records and achievements because you will be able to more effortlessly identify the things that are most relevant for your career and the direction you choose to go.

You are now one step closer to Mastering Your Career Playbook of success!

FINAL THOUGHTS

Bringing it to a Close

I hope that you have found the information contained within this book helpful and that employers will soon start calling your phone repeatedly because you not only possess such impeccable abilities, knowledge and experience; but you've communicated that information properly as well.

Remember that it is not just about getting in the door for the interview, but about getting interviews and receiving the job offer(s) as well!

You may also want to go back and review some of the resumes you have previously submitted for jobs and evaluate those resumes against the information you learned in this book. Going back to review previously submitted resumes will be especially helpful for those positions where you may not have received a follow-up call or phone screen after submitting your resume.

Now that you have this great information at your disposal, think about what you would do differently in submitting your resume when your perfect job becomes available. You may even consider reapplying for a position with your updated, better-crafted resume.

I hope that you will recommend this book to other individuals— students and professionals alike—who can benefit from being more strategic about mastering their career playbook of success.

I would LOVE to receive your input on how this book has helped you within your job search or professional endeavors. Feel free to connect with me on my Twitter at @RegionalConsult, on Instagram @RegionalConsulting or on Facebook at Regional.Consulting.

I look forward to hearing from you soon!!

Juanita

ABOUT THE AUTHOR

Juanita Hines (Speaker |Career Development Specialist | HR & Educational Consultant)

A graduate of North Carolina's esteemed Appalachian State University, Ms. Hines obtained her Bachelors of Science in Communications with a concentration in Public Relations. She has always been dedicated to helping people and encouraging individual and professional empowerment.

With more than ten years of training and development experience, she has been responsible for instructing people on all levels of the employment spectrum within vast industries, levels and professions.

As a former recruiter for one of the DC area's largest- locally owned staffing agencies and a distinguished Contract Recruiter, Ms. Hines has successfully placed professionals ranging from entry-level to C-suite and executive level positions within Fortune 500, government contracting, profit as well as non-profit companies. A few of the clients that she has directly supported includes: The United Negro College Fund (UNCF), BearingPoint,

Booz/Allen/Hamilton, Society of Human Resources Management (SHRM), KPMG, among other internationally recognized corporations and Global Oil & Gas companies.

While she was extremely successful working within Corporate America; Ms. Hines has since made the decision to focus her attention as an HR & Educational Development Consultant; which allows her to go into high schools, colleges, universities, where she offers training empowerment sessions to students and members on a variety of topics ranging from interviewing and resume writing sessions to teaching students about the importance of managing their social media image and making good decisions.

Hines also provides corporate and employee development sessions that are geared towards encouraging professionals to be more strategic in navigating their careers, encouraging employee retention as well as enhancing workplace communication; which are all factors that greatly contribute to employee retention and organizational success.

Through Regional Consulting, Ms. Hines assists and encourages people to strive for their fullest potential and she works to improve the types of positions that can be obtained by offering professional training consultations, empowerment sessions and services that will enhance the quality of life for her clients. Her goal is to impart knowledge in today's youth, students and professionals that will allow them to set insurmountable goals, achieve them and succeed beyond measure.

"As a successful business person and someone who feels compelled to share some of the fruits my experiences and training have allowed, I have made a decision and commitment to be part of the solution rather than complaining about the problem. True empowerment and change can only occur when there is complete transparency and it is my belief that one person can help to make a difference in the world. I have decided to take on that role; by which this responsibility gives definition to our company motto: "Realism-When You Need to Know. "

54394283R00066

Made in the USA
Charleston, SC
03 April 2016